ORTHODOX WORSHIP

*A Living Continuity with the Synagogue,
the Temple, and the Early Church*

Benjamin D. Williams and Harold B. Anstall

Revised and updated

ANCIENT FAITH PUBLISHING
CHESTERTON, INDIANA

Orthodox Worship: A Living Continuity with the Synagogue,
the Temple, and the Early Church
New edition copyright © 2018 Benjamin D. Williams and Harold B. Anstall

Previously published by Light and Life Publishing Company, 1990

Published by:
Ancient Faith Publishing
A Division of Ancient Faith Ministries
P.O. Box 748
Chesterton, IN 46304

All Old Testament quotations, unless otherwise identified, are from the
Orthodox Study Bible, © 2008 by St. Athanasius Academy of Orthodox Theology (published by Thomas Nelson, Inc., Nashville, Tennessee) and are used by
permission. New Testament quotations are from the New King James Version
of the Bible, © 1982 by Thomas Nelson, Inc., and are used by permission.

ISBN: 978-1-944967-54-3

30 29 28 27 26 25 24 23 22 21   18 17 16 15 14 13 12 11 10 9 8 7 6 5 4 3 2

Contents

Preface to the New Edition

THIS REVISED EDITION OF ORTHODOX WORSHIP, coming almost thirty years after its original publication, allows time for reflection on the original work, as well as incorporating any new developments in the field. The original was written for the average layperson—it was not written as a liturgical theology text—and it still stands well as an introductory overview for those interested in the history and development of liturgical worship in the early Church and particularly within Eastern Orthodoxy.

Of note, at the time of its writing the thesis upheld by Fr. Louis Bouyer and Fr. Alexander Schmemann (both specialists in the area of Eucharist and eucharistic liturgy) was not generally accepted. Specifically, they put forward what might be called the "worship thesis," namely that in the first century (before the destruction of the Temple by the Romans in AD 70) the synagogue was a place of worship, not just an assembly hall or center for Torah instruction.

This form of early synagogue worship came forward naturally into early Christian worship, in contrast to the then-prevalent teaching that Christian worship was created from scratch, was characterized by informality and the absence of liturgical forms, occurred in house churches, etc. This worship thesis had its early roots in the work of Alfred Edelsheim, a Jewish convert to Christianity whose ground-breaking work *The Life and Times of Jesus the Messiah* set it forth in 1883.

While not generally accepted in the twentieth century, this

thesis has received more and more support through archaeological excavation, particularly after the 2009 discovery of a synagogue (dating as early as AD 29 and no later than AD 63) at Migdal in Galilee—the home town of Mary Magdalene. In the center of the sanctuary of that synagogue was a stone box covered with symbolic carvings connecting it to the temple in Jerusalem and creating a representation in that local place of worship of the holy place where God resided in the temple. Harry Anstall, my co-author who died in 2002, would have considered this archaeological find to be of the utmost importance, further making the case that Orthodox worship is a living continuity with the synagogue, the temple, and the early Church.

Benjamin D. Williams
December 2018

Introduction

IT IS VERY LIKELY THAT for those not yet Orthodox, the first experience of the Divine Liturgy will be a stunning surprise. This is especially true for the Protestant and others with little or no exposure to liturgical worship. The sudden encounter with the sights, sounds, actions, and aromas of the Divine Liturgy will be new and unfamiliar. It will likely raise questions and may well provoke an inner struggle.

This culture shock is what prompted the authors to write this book. It may well be that reading it will be your first encounter with Eastern Orthodox Christianity—that is, Oriental Christianity. Oriental? It doesn't mean mysterious and weird, but it certainly means "Eastern," as in *oriented*. The dictionary defines *to orient* as:

> To find or fix a position with reference to the east, and hence to all the points of the compass; to cause to face the east exactly; to find the proper bearings or relations of any matter or subject, or to correct one's conception of a thing.[1]

Christianity began in what was then called the Orient, the East— the lands in and around Palestine. And the purpose of this book is to acquaint you with the way in which Eastern Christianity has always worshiped. It is a challenge to look at, to get to know,

---

1   *Funk and Wagnalls New Standard Dictionary of the English Language* (1913), s.v. "orient, to."

to experience, to consider Eastern Christian worship. It is also a challenge to "re-orient" your faith—that is, to turn it toward the East, the source and fountainhead of all Christian faith and worship.

The Divine Liturgy of the Orthodox Church, as we will see, is the original form of Christian worship. It is a product of Eastern Christendom, and until recently its exposure has been limited to the Orthodox churches that were brought to America by immigrants from Eastern European and Middle Eastern countries.[2] These Orthodox churches—Greek, Russian, Serbian, Arab, and others—frequently formed a cultural community that these immigrants brought with them. Thus they were often outside the mainstream of American religious traditions and especially Protestantism.

This historical fact, coupled with a Western mindset that asserts that somehow Reformation and post-Reformation developments within Christianity are more advanced than previous Christian forms and practices, has resulted in the virtually complete isolation of most Protestants from their Orthodox brothers and sisters. It is just this gulf between Eastern and Western Christianity, and specifically the prevailing ignorance and misunderstanding surrounding the Divine Liturgy, that this book hopes to bridge.

Our intent is to explain the background and development of the Divine Liturgy of St. John Chrysostom, the Liturgy that is almost universally used in the Orthodox Church today.[3] Our approach is to address the average Christian. This book is not written for

---

2 The liturgies of Western traditions, including the Roman, Mozarabic, etc., are ultimately traceable to Eastern sources, so far as the essential structure is concerned.

3 Other liturgies in use for special occasions or seasons include the Liturgy of the Presanctified Gifts, the Liturgy of St. Basil the Great, and the Liturgy of St. James the Greater.

people with advanced theological degrees who have studied theology or worship. We will discuss plenty of doctrine and practice in their historical context, but the aim is to help the average person understand what the Liturgy is, how it came to be, and how it came down to us over the course of two thousand years.

Christianity is both faith and practice. It is a process—the ongoing process of growing into the image of Jesus Christ that begins with baptism and the reception of the Holy Spirit. The Divine Liturgy both expresses this relationship and brings the faithful into that ongoing saving relationship with God the Father, made possible by the Son and brought about by the Holy Spirit: it brings them indeed into a deep, personal, and spiritual worship experience before the very Throne of God. Another, secondary purpose of the Liturgy is to instruct those as yet outside the Orthodox Faith in its principal form of worship.

The Divine Liturgy, though, is first and foremost a celebration of worship—one that is transcendent in character. Not just a here-and-now thing, it is worship in the Kingdom of God. It is also considered by many to be the most beautiful and spiritual form of Christian worship. Almost two thousand years of the existence of the Divine Liturgy have resulted in a form and structure of worship that is true to its apostolic origins, while at the same time it has been fine-tuned to accomplish that which is necessary in worship: to transport us into the spiritual realm that we may there bless and offer praises to our God and thereby become what we were created to be.

As Fr. Alexander Schmemann wrote, "The liturgy establishes the reality of the church. Its purpose is not the individual sanctification of its members, but the creation of the people of God as the Body of Christ, the manifestation of the church as the new life in the New Aeon."[4]

---

4   Alexander Schmemann, *Introduction to Liturgical Theology* (Crestwood, NY: St. Vladimir's Seminary Press, 1966), 107.

Our approach to understanding the Divine Liturgy will be topical. Rather than going through the actual Liturgy line by line, we have chosen to focus on the major elements, and the understandings behind them, that make the Liturgy what it is. By doing so we hope to look at and explain the big picture while avoiding the trap of getting lost in the details.

Thus the first two chapters of Part I will explain the historical background of the Liturgy from its foundational elements in Judaism to its early Church origins, and summarize the developments from those origins to the Liturgy's present form. Chapter Three will summarize the Orthodox understanding of worship, which is consistent with that practiced by the early Christian Church. Chapters Four and Five are topical discussions of two doctrines that are crucial to a thorough understanding of the Liturgy and are commonly misunderstood.

Part II is a journey through the Liturgy: a step-by-step unfolding of this great worship form with an explanatory commentary. Finally, a Conclusion summarizes what we have discussed. It is our hope that when you have finished reading this book, you will feel *re-oriented*—that is, turned toward and open to the worship of the Eastern Church. For it is *your* heritage, whether you are Roman Catholic, Eastern Orthodox, or Protestant.

PART I

✠

Understanding
the Divine Liturgy

CHAPTER 1

The Development of
Christian Worship in the Bible

M OST MODERN CHRISTIANS STRUGGLE TO understand why the worship services of the liturgical churches are so different and so structured. Their assumption often is that in New Testament times, worship was spontaneous. The fact is, liturgical worship has its roots in the Scriptures, and all of Christianity worshiped this way for fifteen hundred years. The Eastern Orthodox and Roman Catholic Churches have been worshiping this way—more or less unchanged—for almost their entire life of nearly two thousand years.

Two words need to be kept in mind as one first experiences liturgical worship: *origin* and *changelessness*. Remember, the apostles and the first Christian disciples were Jews. That is, they were Jews who recognized and accepted Jesus Christ as the promised Messiah: they were fulfilled Jews. From their heritage, with its history of liturgical interaction with God, came the Jewish form of biblical worship, which provided the basic structure, the origin of Christian worship. For this reason we see a highly developed Christian liturgical order in use even by the end of the first century—that is, within sixty years of Christ's Resurrection.

The second word is *changelessness*. Perhaps one of the most striking and unique things about Orthodox Christianity, especially in this age of rapid change and even change for its own sake, is its permanence and changelessness. Metropolitan Kallistos Ware wrote that one of the most distinctive characteristics of the Orthodox Church is "its determination to remain loyal to the past, its sense of living continuity with the church of ancient times."[5]

This commitment to protecting the gospel and keeping its message and praise to God the same stems from the conviction that the faith was delivered to us by Jesus Christ, and if we are going to be apostolic, then we have to agree to belong to the same Church that Christ founded. That Church began in the first century, and "there is a sense in which all Christians must become Christ's contemporaries," as John Meyendorff pointed out. He went on to remind us that "the twentieth century is not an absolute norm, the apostolic age is."[6]

C. S. Lewis recognized the changelessness of the Liturgy as an extremely important and very valuable characteristic for practical reasons. He went so far as to say it should be like an old shoe— something that fits, that doesn't have to be broken in all the time, that you don't even notice is there. He concludes these observations by saying, "The perfect church service would be one we were almost unaware of; our attention would have been on God."[7]

As Christianity enters its third millennium, it is characterized among other things by a wide variety of worship practices. The majority of them came into being in the last five hundred years, and surprisingly many are only a couple of hundred years old. So what's so important about worship practices that reach back to

---

5   Timothy Ware, *The Orthodox Church* (New York: Penguin Books, 1963), 203.

6   John Meyendorff, in *Women and the Priesthood*, ed. Thomas Hopko (Crestwood, NY: St. Vladimir's Seminary Press, 1983), 14.

7   C. S. Lewis, *Letters to Malcolm: Chiefly on Prayer* (Glasgow: Collins & Sons, 1964), 6.

the apostolic age and contain the liturgical characteristics C. S. Lewis found so attractive? Beyond changelessness, we'd argue for timelessness.

Why? Because liturgical worship transcends time—and that is one of its purposes. Thus it is a blessing to us moderns that the Orthodox Church has recognized what it has and has resisted change.

Within this changelessness there has indeed been change. But the change has not been in the real nature or substance of the faith and practice of Orthodoxy. Rather, it has been a maturing of and building upon an unchanging core or deposit of the faith. Orthodoxy never changes for change's sake; we only change in order to remain the same. Orthodoxy has always been committed to the exhortation of St. Paul to Timothy to guard the deposit of the faith (1 Tim. 6:20). But at the same time the Church is willing to enhance our practice of worship in order to make it more heavenly, more spiritual, more edifying.

Given all this, however, where did the Divine Liturgy *come from*? What were its origins? How much change has there been over time from the inception of Christian worship in the first-century Jerusalem Church?

We should begin by answering the most basic question: What is liturgy? The word comes from the Greek *leitourgia,* meaning "the work of the people"—that is, the collective work assembled believers do together in offering praise and worship to God. Our understanding of this work will grow as we study the origins of Christian worship practice.

The Old Testament Basis for Christian Worship

Jews at the time of Jesus Christ had already had a history of worship almost fifteen hundred years long. Their history was full of interaction with God, who called them to be His people and who had revealed to them specific instructions as to the offerings and sacrifices involved in His worship. The Bible is clear that God *revealed* to Israel how to worship, and this worship was patterned after things in heaven.[8] These specific forms of worship or liturgies were first seen in the tabernacle of the early Israelites and were consummated in the temple worship that took place later in Jerusalem. The worship of God in the temple in Jerusalem was the first and most prominent focus of Jewish worship. The instructions for this worship delineated the form and frequency of prayer and sacrifice.

Judaism had always practiced a constant cycle of prayers, blessings, and meals—daily, weekly, monthly, and annually. These constituted the second focus of worship for the Jew. The most regular of these cycles were the daily hours of prayer and the annual high feast days. The high feast days included the sacrificial offerings in the temple and were based on Jewish messianic expectation. The meals of these feast days included the breaking of bread and the blessing of the cup. They had parallels with both the temple sacrifice and the messianic feast.

As Fr. Louis Bouyer points out, "The synagogal worship, already before Christ, had its necessary complement in the ritual of the meals: the family meal, and better still at least at the time of Christ, the meals of those communities of the faithful brought together by a common messianic expectation."[9] There was a meal liturgy for the prayers of the meals, and in principle they were required for every meal. However, this liturgy took on the greatest importance in family meals and especially the meals of the holy days. The entire structure of the Last Supper as recorded by St. Luke mirrors the meal liturgy as practiced within Judaism at

---

8   Consider Exodus 12—13, 25—31, Isaiah 6, Daniel 7, and Revelation 4—5, among others.

9   Louis Bouyer, *Liturgy and Architecture* (Notre Dame, IN: Notre Dame Press, 1967), 23.

the time.[10] These meal prayers and their structure contributed directly to the formation of the early Christian celebration of the Lord's Supper.

The third and later focus of worship was that of the synagogue. For the average Israelite, the temple was a place of worship visited only on certain days of the year, and it was most specifically a place of sacrifice. As time went on, the most frequented place of worship became the synagogue, which was comparable to a local church or parish. The synagogue developed a particular form of worship that was patterned on temple worship but without the sacrificial element. These two elements of Jewish worship—synagogue and temple—together provided the basic components of the form or order of the liturgy for the early Christian Church.

This background and its historical development into Christianity is something of which most Christians are ignorant. Even most clergy fail to appreciate and fully understand what Christian worship owes to its Jewish predecessor. In many seminaries, church history seems to start around Pentecost and continue through the end of the first century, from whence it is catapulted into the 1500s. All too many Protestant seminaries have very little coursework in liturgics and liturgical worship, and thus their students gain almost no understanding of the Jewish origins of Christian worship. And most coursework in church history doesn't do justice to the Church's Jewish origins either. However, this deficiency is the result of not adequately understanding liturgics—the study of the origin, development, and meaning of the Liturgy.

Besides the structure or order of worship that came from Judaism into Christianity, we find the origins of the *cycles* of liturgy—the daily, weekly, and yearly cycles of worship—in the Old Testament as well. Again, the earliest Christians were Jews who

---

10   Louis Bouyer, *Eucharist: Theology and Spirituality of the Eucharistic Prayer* (Notre Dame, IN: Notre Dame Press, 1989), 78.

had accepted Jesus Christ as Messiah and as God. How natural for them to continue in the worship pattern God had revealed to them, even as Christ Himself had done, while adding to this pattern elements that were distinctly Christian. In other words, no longer do we sacrifice the blood of bulls and goats, but rather we offer that once-for-all sacrifice of our Lord Jesus Christ, the New Covenant in His Body and His Blood. However, the pattern, the shape of the Liturgy remained essentially the same. Going from Old Covenant to New Covenant, then, did not mean going from liturgy to no liturgy. It meant going from a good sacrifice to a better one within the same basic structure of worship.

We read in Acts 2:46, "So continuing daily with one accord in the temple, and breaking bread from house to house, they ate their food with gladness and simplicity of heart." On a daily basis the apostles continued their Jewish worship practices in the temple, and on a daily basis they broke the bread of Communion. This regularity of time is further confirmed in Acts 3:1, in which Peter and John were going to the temple, because it was the hour of prayer, when they encountered the lame man. Not only did they continue in Jewish worship practice, but they kept the liturgical cycle of daily prayers at set hours of the day as well as the major feast days.

This Old Testament carryover extended to the yearly liturgical feast days as well. We are told in Acts 20:16 that Paul was hastening to return to Jerusalem in order to be there for Pentecost. Since the Holy Spirit was given to us on the Old Testament Feast of Pentecost, that annual feast was carried over into the early Church and remains intact to this day.

Furthermore, we see from the testimony of Scripture that the earliest Christians never had a negative view of the temple. Yes, Stephen criticized the Pharisees for settling for empty temple rituals in place of knowing the living God in the Holy Spirit (Acts 7). But in fact, the earliest Christians continued to worship and gather there, as had their forefathers. St. Luke tells us in Acts 5:12 that all the believers gathered in Solomon's Portico, in the temple. In response to the miraculous healings that were occurring, the apostles were arrested. However, an angel of the Lord released them from jail with the injunction to "Go, stand in the temple and speak to the people all the words of this life" (Acts 5:17–20).

Christian worship, then, was a Christ-centered continuity of order and cycle that continued and preserved the traditional structure of synagogue worship and the meaning of temple worship that the Lord had established in Israel. This basic structure included the Old and New Testament practices of liturgy, baptism, and the Paschal feast, which were transmuted into the Eucharist and certain of the feast days.

The Shape of Temple Worship

The continuity of temple and synagogue worship practices characterized the Church in its earliest days, and the synagogue form became the basic order of worship for the Christian Church. This structure was set very early in the New Testament era while the Church was still seen as essentially a Jewish sect, a messianic sect believing in Jesus Christ.

This order or form of worship was developed even prior to the admission of Gentiles into the Church and before the spread of the gospel outside Judea. Therefore, by the time the Gentile missions began in about AD 38 (and later were enhanced by Paul's missionary activity), this order was established and accepted as the form of Christian worship. Into the basic synagogue form were blended other elements from the temple as well as some uniquely Christian elements.

Regarding the temple, it is important to understand two things about its worship. First, the primary type of activity that took place there was sacrifice. The cadence in the spiritual lives of most

Old Testament Jews was the celebration of the holy feast days with their corresponding offerings.

What determined the manner in which these sacrifices would take place? God had given instructions in Exodus and Leviticus, detailing the manner in which worship is to be offered to God. Secondly, worship in the temple—and in fact all Christian worship—was and is designed to reflect worship in heaven. The Scriptures give us careful glimpses of heavenly worship. We have reports of it in Isaiah 6, Daniel 7, and Revelation 4 and 5. It was on this heavenly worship that the worship of God on earth was patterned.

In Exodus 25—27, we find detailed information about the nature of temple worship, including the physical structure of the temple and its dimensions, instructions for building the ark, the internal décor of the tabernacle, details of the priests' vestments, the use of incense, the presence of an altar, the daily offerings, the use of anointing oil, and the use of images.

Exodus 25 begins the command of God regarding the making of the ark of the covenant. It includes the instruction to make two cherubim of gold, between which God said He would "meet with you, and I will speak with you from above the mercy seat, from between the two cherubim" (v. 22). The mercy seat, or ark of the covenant, was understood as "the empty throne where nothing was to be seen; on this throne God was present—the sole object of worship in Israel. . . . God spoke from between the cherubim—invisibly present on His throne—to Moses, Aaron, Samuel . . . to His people. Here the blood of atonement had been sprinkled each year."[11]

The original ark, which disappeared in the exile, had held the tablets of the Law. It was understood both as the place of sacrifice and the place from which God spoke—the place of communion. Thus in Orthodox churches today, behind the altar on which the

---

11 Bouyer, *Eucharist*, 13.

bread and wine are consecrated to become the Body and Blood of Jesus Christ, who was sacrificed for us, there are representations of two cherubim. Between and before them is the altar at which communion takes place in the Eucharist. Further, on the altar stands a candleholder with seven candles, in the manner of the Jewish menorah, the light of which is the sign of the presence of God.

These elements constituted the revealed manner in which the worship and sacrifice of Israel were to be made to God. Again, the primary function here was that of sacrifice: the offering of an animal to propitiate and atone (make amends or reparation) for the sin of God's people. The belief of the early Church was that the sacrificial death of Jesus Christ and His subsequent Resurrection supplanted all temple sacrifice as a means of propitiation and atonement. In the sacrifice of Himself, Jesus Christ becomes the propitiation for all of mankind's sins; He is the Lamb of God who takes away the sins of the world (John 1:29). Thereafter, for Christians, there was no need for an additional sacrifice. The Good News of Jesus Christ is that our sins are forgiven in Him, and in Him we are reconciled to the Father.

So why continue any of the temple practices? Because they included communion as well as sacrifice, and because they constituted revealed worship—they were part of God's intent from the beginning. Temple worship was fulfilled in Jesus Christ, and thus the worship we offer to God goes on forever. It continues both here on earth and in heaven before the Throne of God. To be specific, heavenly worship is *the* worship, *the* Liturgy. The Church on earth, in spirit and in truth, enters by faith into the Liturgy that is taking place at heaven's throne.

Contrary to what some believe, God the Father and Christ the Son are not just sitting around doing nothing, waiting for the end of time, while the Holy Spirit somehow holds it all together. The scriptural revelation, from Genesis through Revelation, is that worship continually takes place in heaven "before the throne of

God . . . day and night" (Rev. 7:15). That is, heaven is a dynamic condition of praise and worship—of liturgy—to the Father. This is not necessarily worship as we practice it in our human condition, but if we are to believe the Old and New Testaments, it is worship in some transcendent and eternal form.

For example, Hebrews 8 describes the role of Jesus Christ as our heavenly high priest in contrast with the Old Testament priesthood. And what is the word used to describe what our High Priest is doing? It is *liturgy*. The passage properly reads as follows: "We have such a high priest, one who is seated at the right hand of the throne of the Majesty in heaven, a liturgist (*leitourgos*) in the sanctuary and true tabernacle which is set up not by man but by the Lord" (8:1). The worship of heaven, the Liturgy, has been established forever by God himself. Hebrews then goes on to demonstrate that what we do on earth should be patterned after what happens in heaven—in both the Old and New Covenants. "Now Jesus has been given a liturgical work which is superior to theirs, just as the covenant which He arranged between God and His people is a better one" (8:6, literal translation).

According to the Bible, there is worship in heaven, and it is to be our pattern. Some modern translations smuggle in the words "minister" or "ministry," but the original Greek word in every major early text is *leitourgos*. It means "liturgy" or "liturgical worship."

It is easy to understand why the early Christians continued in their synagogue and temple practices. Worship had been revealed to them by God. Nobody thought it up. It didn't just happen. They didn't create a new form of worship. God told His people how to worship. Jesus Christ was the fulfillment of all that God had promised in the Old Testament; in Him all the hopes of Israel were fulfilled. It was only natural that in worshiping God through Jesus Christ, believers would continue to do as they had been told, in the manner God revealed to them.

This was natural, almost automatic, for the Jews who accepted Jesus Christ as Messiah. There was, however, one major change for these Jews who had been completed in Jesus Christ. The animal sacrifices of Old Testament practice had been fulfilled in the person of Christ. All that had been anticipated was now completed. All that had been prophesied was now reality. The Messiah had come. So for these early Christians, the Jewish worship practices were continued with a brand-new understanding of the centrality of the victorious Christ, and with newfound joy.

Christians did not view their Jewish liturgical practices as passé. Nor did they simply continue in some kind of mindless habit of outmoded ritual. They maintained this liturgy as their own, as described in the inspired Scriptures of the Old Covenant carried over into the New. In fact, that Jewish liturgy made the work of God in Jesus Christ comprehensible. The Old Testament worship practices, now fulfilled and given new meaning in Christ, became the core of Christian worship within this New Covenant. The sacrifice had changed, and—thanks be to God—the worship of Jerusalem became available to the whole world. And this worship was centered in Jesus Christ.

The Shape of Synagogue Worship

What then was the basic structure of Jewish worship, and how much of it came into Christianity? Most scholars agree that the structure of Christian worship came almost directly from the synagogue form.[12] The importance of the synagogue to the Jews was due to a historical experience, the Babylonian exile. With no temple in which to worship and sacrifice, faithful Jews were forced to gather around their elders to listen to the Word of God, to receive teaching, and to worship. This form was retained and matured after the return from the exile and became a normal

---

12 Schmemann, *Liturgical Theology*, 52.

part of Jewish religious life. It was patterned on temple worship and was held at the same times as services in the temple.

A brief description of the architecture of the average synagogue in the time of Christ will help us understand these factors. There were three very distinct features to be understood. The first was the seat of Moses. Fr. Louis Bouyer explains:

> The synagogue, the assembly of the People of God, could only meet as such because there was always among them someone held as the authentic depository of the living tradition of God's word, first given to Moses, and able to communicate it anew, although always substantially the same. This then, at the time of Our Lord, was the proper function of the rabbis.[13]

The seat of Moses was represented by seats in the synagogue occupied by the rabbis. These seats were located on a raised platform called a *bema*, which had a central location in the synagogue building.

Each synagogue had an ark that was protected by a veil and before which burned a seven-branched candlestick—the menorah. According to Bouyer,

> The Ark in the synagogue contained the Scriptures and spiritually pointed to the Ark of the Temple, as the physical alignment of the synagogue pointed toward Jerusalem. The ultimate focus of synagogue worship was the Holy of Holies in Jerusalem; just as the focus of worship in the Temple was likewise the Holy of Holies.[14]

We should note that the synagogue was oriented toward Jerusalem, as can be seen in the diagram on the next page.

---

13   Bouyer, *Eucharist*, 13.
14   Bouyer, 13.

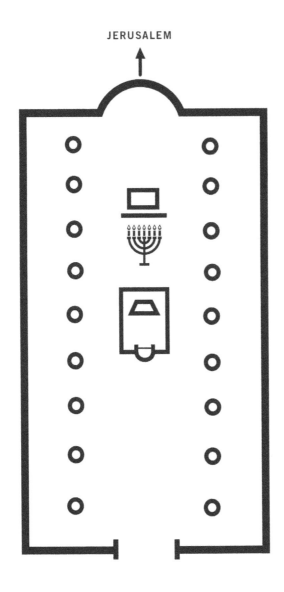

Bouyer's book was published in 1967, and the thesis of early Christian worship modeled on synagogue worship put forward by him and Fr. Schmemann has been substantially supported by more recent archaeological work. The most dramatic discovery involved the excavation of a first-century synagogue at Migdal in Galilee (dated between AD 29 and 63) which unearthed a carved stone box large enough to be the ark sitting in the center of the sanctuary.

That and another similar box in a nearby Byzantine-era synagogue in Horvat Kur are both tied to temple worship in Jerusalem through their carvings. The front panel carries an engraving of the temple's seven-branched menorah; the side panels further connect to the temple with pillared archways; and the back panel depicts two wheels above a geometric shape illustrating fire. This supports not only the contention that the practice in the early Jewish synagogue was a form of worship, but also illustrates that the synagogue acted as a representation of the temple in Jerusalem. It served, according to Rina Talgam at Hebrew University in Jerusalem, to give the space an aura of holiness, "like a lesser temple" even while Herod's Temple still existed.[15]

Luke tells us Jesus went to the synagogue *as was His custom* and was asked to read from the prophet Isaiah (Luke 4:16–30). Alfred Edersheim, in his book *The Life and Times of Jesus the Messiah*, cites the typical order Jesus Himself experienced on the day He began His ministry in Nazareth. He read from the prophet Isaiah that day only because He was requested to by the chief rabbi.

His reading would have been prefaced by antiphonal prayers that began with: *Bless ye the Lord, the One Who is to be blessed,* to which would have been chanted the response: *Blessed be the Lord forever!*

---

15 Isabel Kershner, "A Carved Stone Block Upends Assumptions About Ancient Judaism," *New York Times,* Dec. 8, 2015.

Edersheim describes the event as follows:

On his entrance into the Synagogue, or perhaps before that, the chief ruler would request Jesus to act for that Sabbath as the *Sheliach Tsibbur* (the representative of the people). For, according to the Mishnah, the person who read in the synagogue the portion from the Prophets, was also expected to conduct the devotions. . . . Then Jesus would ascend the Bema and, standing at the lectern, begin the service by two prayers:

Blessed be Thou, O Lord, King of the world, Who formest the light and createst the darkness, Who makest peace, and createst everything; Who, in mercy, givest light to the earth, and to those who dwell upon it, and in Thy goodness, day by day, and every day, renewest the works of creation. Blessed be the Lord our God for the glory of His handiworks, and for the light-giving lights which He has made for His praise. Blessed be the Lord our God, Who has formed the lights.

With great love hast Thou loved us, O Lord our God, and with much overflowing pity hast Thou pitied us, our Father and our King. For the sake of our fathers who trusted in Thee, and Thou taughtest them the statutes of life, have mercy upon us, and teach us. Enlighten our eyes in Thy Law; cause our hearts to cleave to Thy commandments; unite our hearts to love and fear Thy Name, and we shall not be put to shame, world without end. For Thou art a God Who preparest salvation, and hast in truth brought us to hear Thy great Name that we may lovingly praise Thee and Thy Unity. Blessed be the Lord, Who in love chose His people Israel.

After this followed what may be designated as the Jewish Creed, called the Shema, consisting of three passages from the Pentateuch. This prayer finished, he who officiated took his place before the Ark, and there repeated what formed the . . . eulogies or Benedictions. After this, such prayers were inserted as were suited to the day. The liturgical part being thus completed . . . the [chief ruler] approached the Ark and brought out a roll of the Law. On the Sabbath, at least seven persons were called upon successively to read portions from the Law, none of them consisting of less than three verses. Upon the Law followed a section from the Prophets . . . the reading of which was in olden times immediately followed by an address, discourse or sermon.[16]

From Edersheim's description we can see the six basic components in synagogue worship, and with minor differences most scholars agree with his observation.

1. *The Litany.* The first and opening part of the synagogue service was a series of prayers that would have been sung antiphonally—a litany, blessing God for His love toward mankind. In its present form, the Orthodox Liturgy begins with the Great Litany. The celebrant says, "In peace let us pray to the Lord," and the people respond, as they do to each of the following petitions, "Lord, have mercy."

2. *The Confession.* The litany was immediately followed by a confession of God's faithfulness and of mankind's sin. In the Orthodox Liturgy, these may be found in the prayer between the Great Litany and the Scripture reading.

3. *Intercessory Prayer.* The third part was the eulogy, the prayers of intercession. Likewise, these intercessory prayers complement the confessions in preparation for the Scripture readings.

4. *Scripture Readings.* This was followed by the reading from the Law and the Prophets. In today's Orthodox Church, as with any church using a lectionary, these include readings from the

---

16 Alfred Edersheim, *The Life and Times of Jesus the Messiah: Volume II* (London: Longmans & Co., 1899), 436–450.

Old Testament as well as the Epistle and Gospel passages.

5. *Preaching.* The reading was followed by a discourse or sermon that expanded upon the reading and clarified its application to daily life. This is the equivalent of the homily or sermon in modern services.

6. *Benediction.* The service concluded with a benediction, which means "good word."

On the Sabbath, at a time in conjunction with worship in the temple, the assembly gathered around the ark with the rabbi to hear his teaching and to meditate on the Law and the Prophets. We can clearly see that although the synagogue service centered on the reading of the word of God, it did not consist of this exclusively; it also included communion with God in prayer and praise.

> The teaching of the word of God in the synagogue was communion with the most holy presence of the living God among us. That, in the synagogal worship, was emphasized by the fact that, looking at the Ark of Scripture, the Jews were at the same time looking at the Temple, at the dwelling place on earth of (God). There it has been the center of worship, a worship which even then meant a whole life assuming a liturgical character of obedient service in thanksgiving.[17]

This was also one of the forms of worship Jesus practiced. Upon entering the synagogue in Nazareth, Jesus was asked by the ruler of the synagogue to be the liturgist; He participated in the antiphonal litanies that blessed God and began the service. He joined His neighbors in confessing the faithfulness of God. The intercessory prayers were His prayers also. Then, after the reading of the Law, He was asked to read the Prophets. This He did, and then to

---

17 Bouyer, *Eucharist*, 88.

the amazement of those gathered, He did more—He interpreted them. It is unlikely that He heard the benediction, however, given the reaction He received that day.

A fact that cannot be argued with is that for Jesus Christ, the incarnate Word, this was worship. This was His custom, as it was the custom of the disciples and of the Church they were commissioned to build. We cannot get around this continuity in the New Testament.

But what about liturgical worship in the early Church? The question is often asked by modern Christians who want to use the apostolic Church as their model but lack liturgical objectivity. Many, disdaining liturgical worship, hold out for any assertion that liturgy was a late invention of the Church—something sort of dreamt up and introduced after the first century. If we realize that Jewish worship was liturgical and provided the worship structure for the early Church, and then read the New Testament seriously, a whole new side to the question becomes clear.

Reading St. Paul with liturgical eyes, one can see many references to liturgical worship. These include mention of both structure and content. St. Paul did not, of course, write a treatise on liturgy or a description of how worship was to take place. These things were givens—known and practiced in the churches—as is evident in Acts, where St. Luke assumes the reader's knowledge of the basics of Christian worship.

The same is assumed by St. Paul, and we should note his normal missionary practice. In any new city, he went first to the synagogue. Why? To offer the gospel to the Jew first and then to the Gentile. And what would he have done there? The same things we just read about. In fact, it is highly likely that he was frequently (at least in the early years after his conversion) asked, as a visitor and rabbi, to be the liturgist. He would have worshiped as we just saw Jesus did in Nazareth.

The earliest and clearest reference to liturgy comes in Acts, the book that chronicles the inception and growth of the early Church. The church at Antioch was the first Gentile church outside of Jerusalem, established in approximately 38 when Barnabas was sent to teach there (Acts 11:25 ff.). In Acts 13 we learn of the selection of Barnabas and St. Paul for the first missionary journey. This would have taken place in approximately 46, in what by then was a well-established and structured community of believers. Luke records that the calling of Paul and Barnabas was the work of the Holy Spirit and that it took place during the Liturgy. The text reads, "as they were liturgizing (*leitourgounton*) before the Lord and fasting, the Holy Spirit said, 'Set apart for me Barnabas and Saul to the work to which I have called them.'"

Luke was a physician and well educated. We must assume that he understood what he was saying about worship: namely that the community had gathered together in formal and ritual worship, accompanied by fasting, when the Holy Spirit spoke. The reality is, in 46, this early church was worshiping in a liturgical manner, using a Christian form carried over from the synagogue. This was within sixteen years of the Resurrection of Jesus Christ.

As we have seen, the most common translation of *leitourgos* is "the work of the people." It is that common act of God's people together offering praise to Him in the manner He revealed that they should. This was the type of worship that took place in the synagogue and carried over into the early Church. Edersheim goes so far as to say that "the synagogue became the cradle of the Church."[18]

And as if that weren't enough, the components of Jewish worship that came into Christianity did so in the same order. This is evident in that the basic six-point structure of synagogue worship we just saw still constitutes the core of Christian worship, as it has done more or less for two thousand years. This "dependency

---

18   Edersheim, *Life and Times of Jesus*, 55.

of order"[19] verifies the historical and theological truth of the worship practices of the Christian Church as the fulfillment of what God began in Israel.

When you compare it to the form of Christian worship that is conducted on a typical Sunday morning today, you can see that common core. That said, though, there are two major exceptions. First, in most churches, the liturgical aspect is gone—the service has often been reduced to its bare bones of structure. Second, the Eucharist is absent more often than not—the element that for the early Church constituted the whole purpose of the service. Worship was not simply a collection of various parts that struck the fancy of early Christians. Instead, the six major elements of Christian worship were transferred directly from Judaism.

The faith and practice of Orthodox Christianity is in direct continuity with what God began in the Old Covenant and fulfilled in His Son, our Lord Jesus Christ. To remain outside Orthodox Christian worship is to elect to be outside the circle, a Christian unfulfilled in the worship of the New Testament Church.

The Passover

Passover is perhaps the ultimate example of the transformation of a Jewish worship practice into something new and different by Jesus Christ. One of the three major holy days of Israel, Passover celebrated their deliverance by God from the bondage of slavery in Egypt. It included the sacrifice of a lamb in the forecourt of the temple and the partaking of the *seder,* or Passover supper, which included part of the sacrificed lamb. This lamb called to mind the lambs slain in Egypt, their blood brushed on the doorposts and lintels to stay the destroying angel. More than just symbolic, this sacrificed lamb accomplished the deliverance of the people of God for yet another year, while the *seder,* the Passover supper,

---

19 Schmemann, *Liturgical Theology,* 55.

established the reality of communion between God and mankind.[20] That is why every Jew made it a point to be in Jerusalem to celebrate the Passover at least once in his life—only in Jerusalem was it possible to celebrate the Passover completely.

Jesus had entered the city of Jerusalem prior to Passover, desirous of sharing this final supper with His disciples. They asked Him what they must do to prepare for the Passover (John 13:1; Matt. 26:17), and He instructed them to prepare the upper room. The disciples undoubtedly expected to celebrate the actual Passover meal with their Lord, for they were in Jerusalem.

What they were not expecting was what actually took place: Jesus Christ, in the context of a supper, offering Himself as the Lamb of the world. Jesus undoubtedly gathered them for a supper, for all the Gospels record it. But what is important to recognize is that the supper Jesus and His disciples celebrated together was not the *seder* supper of Passover. It certainly was a supper in the context of Passover, and the types of the Passover festival were present, including the breaking of bread and the drinking of the cup; but it was not the actual Passover *seder,* because it took place on Thursday evening. The Passover *seder* would have had to be celebrated on Friday evening, at the beginning of the Jewish Sabbath, and in this case the beginning of the Days of Unleavened Bread.

The significance of this is that because the supper took place on Thursday night, the day before Passover, there was no slaughtered lamb from the temple to partake of. Without the sacrificed lamb from the temple, the meal would not be a *seder.* According to St. John, the death of Christ took place the next day, Friday, while the lambs were being sacrificed in the temple (18:28). Thus, the Last Supper is an anticipation of the sacrifice of Golgotha rather than an actual Passover meal. Jesus was crucified on Golgotha

---

20   Van Orelli, "Passover," *The Schaff-Herzog Encyclopedia of Religious Knowledge* (1888).

the following day, on Friday, in order that the Jewish authorities could complete His death before the Sabbath and the beginning of Passover on Friday evening.

Luke tells us that Jesus told the disciples at the table, "With *fervent* desire I have desired to eat this Passover with you before I suffer; for I say to you, I will no longer eat of it until it is fulfilled in the kingdom of God" (Luke 22:15). Jesus Himself said that He would not eat another Passover until it had been fulfilled in the Kingdom; therefore what He and the disciples ate must not have been a Passover meal. "Our Lord gathered His disciples for a ritual meal, which was the same as the prayer of sacrificial representation in the temple."[21] Jesus did not intend to eat Passover with His disciples in Jerusalem, for He knew that He was the Lamb to be sacrificed on Friday.

The lambs being slaughtered in the temple are of the Old Covenant; the Lamb being sacrificed on the Cross is the New Covenant in Jesus Christ, the fulfillment of the Law and the Prophets. Jesus Christ, in the offering of His Body and His Blood, is the sacrificial Lamb. Rather than sharing lamb from the temple to accomplish their deliverance for yet another year, Jesus was offering Himself, in whom they and all the world would be delivered from sin and death.

Our Lord Himself took a specific Jewish worship practice—one that had been revealed by God—filled it with the new meaning of the New Covenant, and transformed it into Christian Communion. He had become the Passover Lamb, ready to be sacrificed for the deliverance of God's creation. And while the Eucharist was instituted for the Twelve within the context of the Passover Feast, it was not instituted at a Passover meal. In this Jesus actualized the Church and brought it into being.[22] Is it any wonder that the early Christians thought of the Eucharist as delivering them from

---

21 Bouyer, *Eucharist*, 23.
22 Schmemann, *Liturgical Theology*, 63.

death (bestowing life) and establishing communion with God (unity in Christ)? Deliverance and communion were the focus of the Passover, which had now been refocused in Christ Himself.

The problem with understanding the Last Supper as the Passover *seder,* and by extension of understanding the Eucharist as a re-presentation of the Last Supper, is that it results in the observance becoming a dramatic memorial. The Last Supper was a historical event that occurred once. In contrast, the Eucharist is the actual experience of the Lamb who was eternally offered on the Cross.

True, the crucifixion occurred once in time and need not occur again, as the New Testament clearly states. But the crucifixion of Christ is an event with eternal consequences. Through this event, all humankind both before and after the Cross—in fact all creation—may be saved. In this sense it is an eternal sacrifice. Not that Christ is eternally re-sacrificed, but that the scope of the crucifixion is eternal—reaching out to each of us in the Eucharist.

That is why in the Orthodox prayer before Communion, the priest says, "remembering . . . the cross, the tomb, the resurrection on the third day, the ascension into heaven, the sitting at the right hand, and the second and glorious coming." What do we remember? Those actions of Jesus Christ that are eternal (past, present, and future), that transcend time and space, and in which we are saved to eternal life. The Eucharist is the actualization of the Cross, the Tomb, the Resurrection, and the Second Coming.

CHAPTER 2

Worship in the Early Church

S O, THE EARLY BELIEVERS IN Christ continued in the traditions
of their Jewish forefathers, worshiping as they had in both the
temple and the synagogue. To this worship practice they added
distinctly Christian components, which were in fact transformed
Jewish worship practices. These included baptism, the Eucharist,
the *agape* meal, and others. Baptism was also present in Jewish religious practice as a personal repentance for sin. It, like the
Lord's Supper, was transformed in both meaning and content by
our Lord Jesus Christ. Baptism became not only a repentance
for one's sins: being baptized in the name of the Trinity now also
assured forgiveness and incorporation into the Body of Christ, the
Church. Baptism was the once-and-for-all initiatory rite whereby
one received the Holy Spirit and came into the Church.

The early Christians, with their transformed understanding
of the central elements of Judaism, had a practical problem: How
should they conduct their worship? How could they carry on their
old Jewish worship practices while at the same time incorporating this new meaning and content? They accepted the necessity
for continuity with the old and celebration of the new but could
not do both together.

The result was doing both in parallel. The temple hours of
prayer and the synagogue worship were kept but were not centered

in Christ. Each day of the week, those Christian believers in Jerusalem would attend the temple for prayers during the daily cycle, and on Saturday—the Jewish Sabbath—they would attend either temple or synagogue. But what to do about the Eucharist? It could not be added to a synagogue service, yet it was to be celebrated as the Lord had commanded.

The answer was tied to the Resurrection. Jesus had been crucified on Friday, the day before the Jewish Sabbath, and had risen on Sunday, the third day. Thus the day after the Sabbath was seen as the day of the Lord's Resurrection, the Lord's Day. At the Lord's Supper, the *parousia,* or presence of Jesus Christ, was experienced in the consecrated Gifts; here people encountered Christ's new life in His Resurrection. It was only natural that the Eucharist or Lord's Supper should be celebrated each Resurrection Day.

Thus, the typical pattern for early believers became synagogue worship on the Sabbath, followed by gathering for the Lord's Supper on the next day. For the Jews, the day ended at sundown and the next day began. Sunday began at nightfall on Saturday. As Luke records in Acts 20:7, "On Saturday evening we gathered together for the fellowship [Communion] meal" (NEV). The pattern typically became one of worshiping in synagogue on the Sabbath morning and then gathering together again in the evening (the next day—Sunday) for the celebration of the Lord's Supper.

In the early Church, the Lord's Supper was celebrated at the end of the *agape* (love) or fellowship meal. This was an extension of the Passover supper tradition and was a means for believers to show one another the love and unity they shared together in Christ. All gathered and brought what they could. At the conclusion of the meal was the Eucharist, the thanksgiving for the grace of Jesus Christ. The sacrament conveyed the understanding and symbolism of the Passover supper, now consummated in the Body and Blood of Jesus Christ, the Lamb of God. It is highly probable that it was the absence of this Jewish understanding that accounted for the disintegration and abuse of the *agape* meal in the Gentile churches. Paul berates the Corinthians for being self-ish, causing some to go hungry, and for drunkenness at the meal which became so pervasive that it even prevented the Eucharist from being celebrated (1 Cor. 11:20–21).

What we see, however, especially during the early years prior to the Gentile missions, was a link between these old and new worship practices. A Jewish male who became a follower of the Way would have been circumcised as a child, and with his wife and family would continue in the normal Jewish worship pattern with a new Christian understanding. The early Church proceeded in this manner until the Gentile missions brought into the Church people without a Jewish tradition, raising the sort of problems we have just noted. However, in the earliest days of the Church converts were expected to become Jews as well as Christians, and males were expected to be circumcised. This in itself speaks strongly of continuity with Jewish worship practice. It was the persecutions that shook this coexistence and steered Jewish Christian practice toward a more distinctly Christian form of worship.

The first persecution, recorded in Acts 6 and 7, involved the martyrdom of St. Stephen. The early persecutions were by the Jews, who saw the early Church as a heretical sect that was winning converts from Judaism. With the persecutions, the life of the Church was changed: it was excluded from Judaism. And that meant exclusion from Jewish worship; Christians were no longer able to gather in the synagogue and were unwelcome in the temple as well. For example, in Acts 21 St. Paul is mobbed within the temple grounds. The active Jewish persecutions excluded Christians from the temple and forced them toward new worship traditions.

What was this resulting Christian order? The synagogue worship structure consisted of a litany of prayers, a confession, eulogies, readings from the Scriptures, an address or homily, and a benediction. This form constituted the core of what was to become specifically Christian worship.

Evidence for this can be found in archaeological evidence from the earliest Syrian churches, as well as in the *Apostolic Constitutions* and the *Didache*, and in the continuing practices of the Nestorian churches. "The old Syrian church appears as a Christianized version of a Jewish Synagogue."[23] There is a bema in the center, an ark with veil and candle to hold the Word of God, and a seat for the bishop that is representative of the seat of Moses. To these synagogue elements was added an altar, and the church now had an orientation. The architectural arrangement can be seen in the illustration on the next page.

There is a very specific reason for the eastward orientation of Christian churches, one that in some senses is similar to the facing of Jewish synagogues toward the temple in Jerusalem. Christians look to the heavenly Jerusalem from which the Messiah will come, and know themselves to be the "temple of the Holy Spirit." However, the east is the place of the rising sun, and for early Christians was "the only fitting symbol of the last appearance of Christ in His *parousia*, as Sun of Justice in Zecharia."[24] Tertullian speaks of public and private prayer facing toward the east as being an apostolic tradition. It expressed the eschatological expectation that Christ will appear as the Rising Sun that will never set.

To the core synagogue structure (commonly referred to as the *synaxis* or the Liturgy of the Word) was added the fulfilled temple worship, the Eucharist, which was inserted prior to the benediction. This included the use of sung or chanted psalms, which were part of Jewish worship and to which St. Paul refers in Ephesians 5:19 and Colossians 3:16 when he encourages the use of psalms, hymns, and spiritual songs. Again, St. Paul's missionary approach demonstrates this connection, for his approach in any

---

23   Bouyer, *Eucharist*, 25.
24   Bouyer, 28.

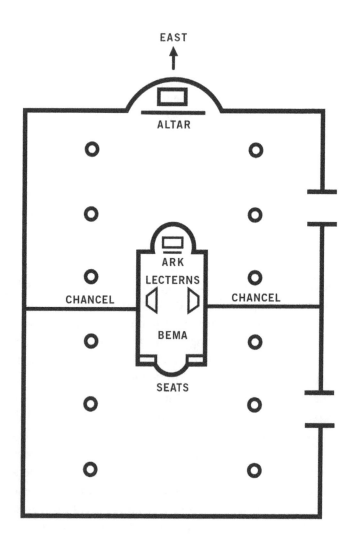

new city was to worship first in the synagogue, using that base for proclaiming the gospel. The Jerusalem church was the mother church for early Christianity, to which the Church at large looked for guidance in all things theological and liturgical. The missionary churches naturally followed the form of the Jerusalem church. Thus the Gentile churches that came into being as a result of St. Paul's preaching and teaching had this same Jewish rule of prayer, or order of worship. The similarity to the synagogue ritual within the first-century Church demonstrates an early universal acceptance of Jewish worship origins.[25]

Eusebius, a fourth-century historian and bishop, in his book *The History of The Church* (18.1), quotes Philo, a Jewish historian writing in the first century. Philo describes the *Christian* "all-night vigils of the great festival, the spiritual discipline in which they are spent, the hymns that we always recite, and how while one man sings in regular rhythm the others listen silently and join in the refrains of the hymn."[26] This is antiphonal singing of litanies, and it certainly reflects Jewish worship practice, which Philo recognizes. By the end of the first century, the Christian Church was present throughout much of the empire. There were established churches in most of the major cities and in many smaller ones. These churches continued following the order of Jewish worship—essentially the synagogue liturgy with the inclusion of the Eucharist. But the typical worship of the first and second centuries was of necessity simple. The Church was generally under persecution, so it tended to hold its worship services in secret, usually in the homes of members. As Fr. Schmemann states, the liturgical form was commonly "the bishop, surrounded by presbyters [elders] facing the assembly, the Supper Table, on which the deacons placed the gifts [bread and wine] which were

---

25 Schmemann, *Liturgical Theology*, 154.
26 Eusebius of Caesarea, *The History of The Church from Christ to Constantine* (New York: Dorset Press, 1984), 93.

being offered, preaching, prayer, the anaphora [prayer before Communion] and the distribution of the Holy Gifts."[27]

The freedom of the first years of the Church's life, in which she could be liturgically Jewish in synagogue and temple and also celebrate the Eucharist, was gone. What is evident is a liturgical contraction under the duress of persecution. By now the "unnecessary" material of the synagogue service had been compressed or even dispensed with. What was left was a simpler service focused on the Eucharist, but one that still reflected the synagogue form and contained its major elements.

But we cannot take this liturgical contraction to imply that the early Church was primitive, had no ceremony, and subscribed to simple beliefs. In his introduction to *The History of The Church*, G. A. Williamson says of Eusebius that in his own statements and those of the earliest authorities on which Eusebius draws we see a Church that we would recognize as our own.

> We shall find the same line drawn between clergy and laity, the same division of the clergy into the three orders of bishops, presbyters, and the deacons, the same practice of Episcopal ordination and consecration, the same insistence on Apostolic Succession and on the establishment by Christ of One Holy Catholic and Apostolic Church. We shall find Christendom partitioned up into dioceses and archdioceses, presided over and ruled by bishops who are held in the highest esteem.[28]

Focused on the Eucharist

By the second century, the Lord's Supper (or Eucharist) began to be separated from the *agape* meal. Differing opinions exist as to whether this was due to problems such as those in Corinth or the

---

27 Schmemann, *Liturgical Theology*, 119.
28 Eusebius, *History of the Church*, 9.

increasing presence in the Church of Gentiles, who lacked a Jewish perspective. The net result was the celebration of the Eucharist without the *agape* meal.

The word *Eucharist* means "thanksgiving" or "the giving of thanks" (see Luke 22:16). At the Last Supper, the institution of the Eucharist, Christ's intent was not on the perpetuation of a mere meal or Passover supper. Instead, that meal was fulfilled in the partaking of the Body and Blood of Jesus Christ. And it is after the Resurrection, the Ascension, and Pentecost that the incredible significance of the Eucharist comes to light, for the Lord, who gave the Church this sacrament, is risen and ascended. He is the living Lord Jesus Christ, who reigns at the right hand of God the Father. He said not only, "This is My Body and Blood," but He also told His followers, "Most assuredly, I say to you, unless you eat the flesh of the Son of Man and drink His blood, you have no life in you" (John 6:53). One cannot get around this point in Scripture.

The early Christians took their Lord at His word, believing that in a mystery bread and wine became the Body and Blood of Jesus Christ, and that it was life-giving. That is, through the work of the Holy Spirit, each believer was nurtured by grace (sacramentally) and received spiritual sustenance. Behind this understanding of the nature of the Eucharist was the understanding of worship held by the entire early Church. As Fr. Schmemann tells us,

> The worship of the church has at its real center the constant renewal and repetition in time of the one unchanging Sacrament: unchanging that is in its meaning, content and purpose. But the whole significance of this repetition is in the fact that something unrepeatable is being recalled and actualized. The Eucharist is the actualization of one single, unrepeatable event.[29]

---

29 Schmemann, *Liturgical Theology*, 43.

This is readily apparent in the portion of the Liturgy or Mass before Communion—the memorial that remembers, that "re-presents every Sunday the saving death of Christ in the expectation of the resurrection. . . . The Eucharistic meal has taken the place of the former sacrifices. No other sacrifice can have any meaning but the cross of Christ, celebrated in the Christian meal. Through it, while taking part in His passion, we are being given a foretaste of His resurrection."[30]

These liturgical actions—and the faith of the early Christians—focus on the Body and Blood of Christ. More specifically, they bring the biblical promise of the reality of His sacrifice for us—made available in these gifts—and the reality of spiritual nurture. Ultimately, it is a question of life. Jesus said He came that we could have life and have it more abundantly. He also said He would send His Spirit, the Spirit of Life, to transform us and all creation, to set us apart.

The belief of the early Church was that the Eucharist was this transforming life—spiritual life. It was not a Christian snack or a trip down memory lane with the Lord. It was a miraculous experience of the grace of God in the Holy Spirit.

This was certainly the belief of Justin Martyr, circa AD 150, who said, "For we do not receive these things as though they were ordinary food and drink. . . . The food over which the thanksgiving has been spoken becomes the flesh and blood of the incarnate Jesus in order to nourish and transform our flesh and blood." St. Justin called this food "Eucharist," thanksgiving, or "blessing," just as he called baptismal washing "enlightenment." For him this was a real and powerful act of God.[31]

The question that has to be faced by contemporary Christians is a simple one: Is this sacrament simply symbolic, or are the

---

30   Bouyer, *Eucharist*, 32.
31   Raymond Johanny, ed., *The Eucharist of the Early Christians* (New York: Pueblo Publishing Co., 1990), 75.

bread and wine changed into spiritual and life-giving nourishment provided by our Lord? One doesn't have to get into a theological debate about transubstantiation or other technical ways of explaining the sacrament. The statement about the Eucharist has traditionally been that this is the Body and Blood of Jesus Christ by which we are spiritually fed.

Thus, for us now as for the apostles then, the biblical promise is that by believing on Jesus Christ as Lord and Savior and being baptized in the name of the Holy Trinity, we receive new life in that sacrament through the indwelling of the Holy Spirit. And as we partake of the Body and Blood of Jesus Christ in the Eucharist, we continue to receive new life in Christ through the grace of the Holy Spirit. This indeed is something for which to give thanks, hence the name *Eucharist*, thanksgiving. And this was the uniform view of the early Church. Saint Ignatius, who died in AD 107, "thought of the Church as a Eucharistic society which only realized its true nature when it celebrates the Supper of the Lord, receiving His Body and Blood in the Sacrament."[32]

Gregory Dix, in his classic treatise on the development of liturgical worship, states that in the earliest accounts of the Eucharist, the Church places the words of institution centrally in the eucharistic prayer. He goes on to point out that it used formulas that were in keeping with those of John's Gospel, "that Bread which cometh down from Heaven and giveth life unto the world, he that *eateth* of this Bread *shall live for ever*."[33] He then quotes St. Ignatius, who had described the eucharistic bread as "a remedy bestowing immortality, an antidote preventing death and giving life in Jesus Christ."

That this was indeed the belief of the early Church can also be seen in how they worshiped. We have observed how the early

---

32 Ware, *The Orthodox Church*, 21.

33 Dom Gregory Dix, *The Shape of the Liturgy* (New York: The Seabury Press, 1983), 137.

Christian Church may be seen as a christological synagogue. For the majority of the service the bishop would be seated on the bema or stand thereon. The ark had become in the Syrian church the place where the Gospel book was "enthroned," and this was probably so throughout the early Church. The Word was taken from the ark and proclaimed from the bema, and by it the believer was led to the altar and beyond it to the Kingdom.

This happened literally as well as spiritually. There were no pews in the early Church. This practice continued almost universally up until the seventeenth century in the West and is still maintained in most Orthodox churches outside of America today. Upon the completion of the prayers and Scripture readings, the clergy would take the bread and wine and proceed to the east—to the altar for the eucharistic meal. The vital nature of the early Christian worship is expressed in this procession toward the east (that is, the Kingdom). "Therefore the whole assembly, far from being a static mass of spectators, remains an organic gathering of worshipers, first centered on the ark, for hearing and meditating upon the Scriptures, and finally going toward the East all together for the Eucharistic prayer and the final communion."[34]

This movement toward the altar with the Gifts is the origin of what is now called in the Divine Liturgy the Great Entrance, when the clergy bring the bread and wine from the preparation table to the altar before the Eucharist; of this we will learn more in Part II. The only major change over time in the structure of this portion of the Liturgy was the movement of the Gospel into the sanctuary, before the altar, in advance of its being read to the assembled congregation. In part, once again, this was due to the circumstances the Church experienced. For the early Church, the Gospel book was of inexpressible value, for it was the Word of Life. One of the common goals of the persecuting Romans was to confiscate and destroy the Gospel book. Thus, along with the sacred vessels, it

---

34 Bouyer, *Eucharist*, 35.

was kept in a safe place during the week, and only brought out for the service of the Divine Liturgy. This circumstance would have existed through the early part of the fourth century, changing only with the end of the persecution of Diocletian.

What transpired then was the assembling of believers before the Liturgy began, typically singing psalms of praise in anticipation of communion with God. The clergy would arrive bearing the Gospel book and the sacred vessels and enter the Church, carrying the Gospel book to the center of the building (onto the bema in the very earliest churches). Then, after the reading of the Gospel lesson to the assembly, the Gospel book would be carried to the altar. From this real experience has come two portions of the Orthodox Divine Liturgy: the Antiphons and the Little Entrance. The Antiphons (two or three are commonly sung) are composed of psalms which are sung antiphonally by cantor and choir or congregation. These go back to the psalms sung by the assembled congregation while awaiting the arrival of the clergy and echo the psalms chanted antiphonally in the Jewish synagogue.

The Little Entrance is the bearing of the Gospel into the sanctuary, and it likewise can be traced to the carrying of the Gospel book into the church. With the end of persecution, it could be kept in the church, and until recent times, the practice was for the Gospel to be in the middle of the church at the beginning of the Divine Liturgy, and from there to be carried into the sanctuary during the Little Entrance, to be read before the altar. Having been brought into the midst of the assembly, the Book of Life is then carried into the sanctuary, where through the Gospel of Jesus Christ, all of the assembly enter into the Kingdom to partake of the Eucharist.

We have seen that Bishop Ignatius of Antioch referred to the Church as a "eucharistic community" who realizes her true nature when she celebrates the Eucharist. His view of the Church was the local community gathered around its bishop, celebrating the Eucharist. It is important to note that St. Ignatius became Bishop of Antioch in AD 67—in the midst of the New Testament era, while most of the apostles were still alive and active. Saint Ignatius was the second bishop of Antioch, succeeding St. Peter. Thus, we can safely trust that this understanding of the nature of the Church and the Eucharist was representative of that held by the apostles and the Church at large.

By the end of the first century the basic form or order of the Liturgy was established and universally celebrated throughout the Christian Church, though with regional and cultural differences in expression. The Liturgy had as its center the worship of Jesus Christ and the partaking of His Holy Gifts. In the process she remained true to her origin in Jewish worship, which the Lord Himself had practiced and which had been revealed by God. At the core was no longer the shed blood of bulls or goats. This sacrifice was fulfilled for all time in the Body and Blood of Jesus Christ, which is central still to the life of the Church in the Holy Eucharist. Thus, as the lives of the apostles ended, as the responsibility for the Church was being handed on to the next generation, her worship of God was established. The basic form of the Liturgy was settled, to be refined and enhanced over the coming years but never altered in its basic form and meaning.

There is a common accusation leveled against liturgical worship: that liturgical worship is too ritualistic and that its structure stifles the true expression of the people of God and limits the work of the Holy Spirit. What do we say to this? Let us simply recall that the Greek word for liturgy is *leitourgia*, which means "work of the people." As we have seen, *liturgy* is also often translated to mean "worship." In its Christian context, liturgy is all of that and something more. It is the work of the people, because all of the people do indeed work together to offer their worship, praise, and thanks to God. But it is also "an action by which a group of people become something corporately which they had not been as a mere collection of individuals—a whole greater than the sum of its parts."[35]

Liturgy, then, is that celebration of the Church, which has its origins in God's revelation, by which believers worship God and in the process are formed into the Church. That is why the Eucharist is the focal point of the Liturgy: it is in the Eucharist that we receive new life by the grace of God.

Beginning in the fourth century a number of major historical and cultural events impacted the Church, all of which affected the Liturgy as well as the practice of the faith. As we consider these events, remember that the basic structure of the Liturgy had been established; future changes occurred within the framework of that basic shape. The persecutions that the Christian Church experienced began in Palestine with the persecution by the Jews; they continued when Rome herself began to persecute the followers of the Way. The persecutions waxed and waned depending upon the current emperor and the need for political scapegoats. In this polytheistic society Christianity was even accused of atheism for its worship of only one God. The persecutions forced the Church underground. There are in fact two references in the text of the Liturgy still used today that hearken back to those days of persecution and secrecy. During those years the Church lived within a society that was against it formally and informally, actively and passively.

The Conversion of Constantine

Although he was not baptized until just prior to his death in AD 337, Constantine embraced Christianity, made it legal, and for all practical purposes made it the religion of the state. With

---

35 Alexander Schmemann, *For the Life of the World: Sacraments and Orthodoxy* (Crestwood, NY: St. Vladimir's Seminary Press, 1973), 25.

the Edict of Milan in AD 313 he granted free religious worship and recognition by the state. As a result, the persecution of the Church finally ended, as did the need for secrecy. This caused the first of the major changes in the form of the Liturgy.

The persecutions of the Church during the previous two hundred years had waxed and waned, depending upon the emperor and his orientation; there were periods of relative peace and tolerance, and periods of active persecution and martyrdom. During these periods of tolerance the Church flourished, privately and publicly. Yet, as an illegal entity within the state, it could not really grow and flower in any large-scale fashion. With the acceptance brought about by Constantine, all this changed. Now it became possible to publicly erect churches dedicated to the worship of God, and to do so with state support. Christian worship became a public affair, and these changes not only ended the liturgical contraction that occurred under persecution but also resulted in an elaboration of the ceremonial aspect of worship. Christian worship was now being seen by nonbelievers; thus it was not only necessary that it be understandable to them but also that the necessary sense of reverence and thanksgiving be conveyed. Worship had always been corporate; now it became public. In addition, worship began to take on an understanding of having a missionary and proclamation role to fulfill that it had not had before. All of this resulted in a more literal understanding of the *do* in Christ's words "Do this in remembrance of Me." The result was a greater focus on action and ceremony within worship.[36]

These enhancements in act and ceremony manifested themselves in a variety of ways. The Church had always worshiped in homes, but during times of toleration, it began taking over secular buildings and converting them for Christian worship. The new public places of worship were larger, and there was

---

36 Dix, *Shape of the Liturgy*, 397.

amplification of the service over what had been celebrated in earlier times. Clerical vestments began to appear. The use of chanting and hymnody, having their basis in Jewish worship, became more highly developed in this more public worship and proclamation. There was a heightened sense of drama, with entrances, processions, and censing,[37] also built upon Old Testament worship. The use of icons as a means of remembering Christ and His saints and martyrs became more widespread. These changes occurred in response to the cultural change that the Church was experiencing with the end of persecution and its open acceptance within society.

Perhaps nothing better illustrates this process than the development of clerical vestments. The most striking aspect of the development of vestments is that they came out of everyday culture. In the early church, in fact, there was a marked attitude that there should be no liturgical vestments, that the celebration of worship and of the Eucharist should take place in everyday dress. This was in spite of the fact that Exodus 28 describes clerical vestments to be worn by the priests. With the exception of the use of a stole as a sign of office, all dressed alike in street clothes. Saint Gregory of Nazianzus records between AD 375 and 400 that there was "no difference between clerical and lay dress."[38] This sign of office was present early on, for Polycrates, Bishop of Ephesus, refers in AD 190 to the Apostles John and James who "became sacrificing priests wearing the mitre."[39]

The clothing of the day derived from the normal and traditional clothing worn in Greek and Roman society. What brought about the changes in clothing within the Church was what began to happen within society. "What turned this clothing into a special liturgical vesture was mere conservatism. When the dress

---

37 Schmemann, *Liturgical Theology*, 120.
38 Dix, *Shape of the Liturgy*, 399.
39 Eusebius, *History of the Church*, 141.

of the layman finally changed in the sixth and seventh centuries to the new barbarian fashions, the clergy as the last representatives of the old civilized tradition retained the old civilized costume."[40] Again, a change within the culture had resulted in a favorable liturgical change within the Church. Dix goes on to point out that to this "accidental" distinction that developed between lay and clerical clothing added "symbolic enrichment," adding Christian meaning to things that had utilitarian origins. This also included the use of lights and censing during the Eucharist.[41] Again, we see elements of Old Testament worship being retained and in fact taking on new meaning in the worship of the New Covenant.

We must not take lightly the beauty and aesthetic aspect of worship. Anyone who has walked into a large and solemn church, especially one that is old or of a liturgical tradition, knows the natural sense of reverence found therein. We all want to be beautiful people, to live in beautiful homes; we prefer the aesthetically pleasing to the crass. Should we expect anything less in worship, when we enter into deep communion with our God, who created all things in beauty? Christian worship is a thing of the Kingdom of God and is to show forth the Kingdom—spiritually and symbolically—hence the natural desire to make worship and the church itself both beautiful and aesthetically appealing. Fr. Schmemann writes of the development of the Divine Liturgy:

> The faith and experience of the Church are inseparable from Scriptures, which are its source. Everything the Church believes and by which it lives took place 'according to the Scripture' . . . But this 'according to the Scripture' means much more than fulfillment of prophecies and predictions; it means first of all the inner link between what Christ did

---

40 Dix, *Shape of the Liturgy*, 404.
41 Dix, 430.

and what the Scripture relates—aside from this link neither Scripture nor the meaning of Christ's acts can be understood. The unfolding and deepening reflection of this link is precisely the content of the Christian service, of Church poetry, and even of the rite itself.[42]

Notice the three key words in this observation. The first, obviously, is *Scripture*. It is and must be the basis of all the Christian is and does. The second key word is *unfolding*. Just as theology and doctrine (the understanding of *why* and *what* we believe) took many centuries to develop, so did the *unfolding* of the form of worship require a similar amount of time to unfold and blossom. The third key word is *deepening*. For anything in life to become filled with meaning and value requires time. The process of Christian worship itself moving beyond the immediate and the obvious to the meaningful and deep (i.e., "the width and length and depth and height" of the faith [Eph. 3:18]) required time. And the process of this natural development also included the desire to make worship beautiful.

This is important to grasp as we consider the process by which the Liturgy developed. We have seen how Christian worship made the natural transition from Jewish worship forms to Christian. Under Constantine, Christian worship and especially the Divine Liturgy continued to change. The result is a form of Christian worship almost two thousand years old, one that naturally developed under the guidance of the Holy Spirit and matured to be all that it could be. How do we account for its beauty and splendor other than by this process and by the Church's desire that the Liturgy be a reflection of heavenly worship?

We have seen how clerical vestments came into being, both to preserve the old dress traditions and to show forth the glory

---

42 Alexander Schmemann, *The Historical Road of Eastern Orthodoxy* (Crestwood, NY: St. Vladimir's Seminary Press, 1963), 191.

of the Kingdom. Another architectural illustration may help us appreciate the significance of what was now occurring within the Christian Church. The most common form for large public buildings in the Roman Empire was the basilica. Essentially a large rectangle, the span of its roof was held up by two rows of pillars running the length of the building. This form was common in buildings that had been erected for secular purposes and were then taken over for Christian worship, demonstrating that the building itself was not the most important aspect of the temple. It remained the most common form of church architecture in the West through the Renaissance. The illustration below shows two common forms.

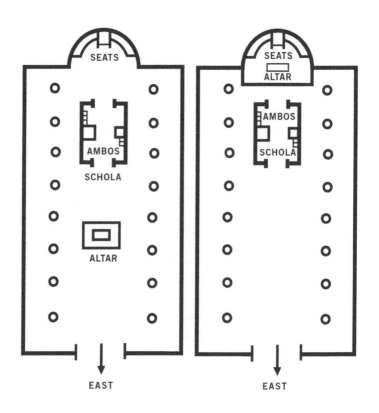

The basilica had inherent limitations. First, the two rows of columns divide the inner space of the Church into three sections, and so the assembly is divided into three sections. Only the center portion could house a united congregation; the result was three congregations. In larger basilicas with subdivisions, the result could be five separate groupings. In addition, the length of the basilica resulted in a further separation due to the distance from the rear to the altar. For the early Byzantine architects, beginning under Constantine, these problems were solved by developing a building where everything was there for a specific purpose.

The most dramatic aspect of this architectural development was replacing the rectangular building with a square one with no columns but with a dome atop it to cover the span. The bema with the ark, the lectern, and bishop's seat could be centrally located

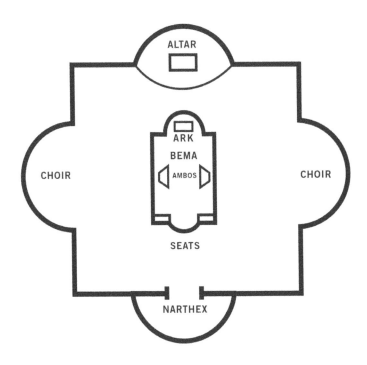

with no hindrance to the believers assembling around the bishops and readers for the synaxis. The assembly would then open for the procession of the Holy Gifts to the altar and rearrange itself so as to be gathered around the altar. It is easy to see from the diagram above how this architectural arrangement would enhance worship.

The Church of Hagia Sophia (Holy Wisdom), begun by Constantine, "would become the grandiose model of the new type of Christian church, which may be the best adaptation to its primary purpose ever achieved in the past."[43]

The Byzantine Empire

The other major cultural event affecting the development of the Divine Liturgy was the founding of the Byzantine Empire. After becoming emperor, Constantine established a new capital for the empire in AD 330 in the ancient fishing town of Byzantium and gave it the name Constantinople. Situated on the Bosphorus in present-day Turkey, the city is now known as Istanbul. It was this new city which was to become the center of the Byzantine Empire. This process would take time and be influenced by the social and political realities of the day, but here was to develop the center and pinnacle of art and culture for the next thousand years.

Constantine conceived of a theocracy, where the emperor ruled the empire on behalf of and for God, was the protector of the faith, and ensured the well-being of the citizens. His conception was the sunlight and water that allowed the Church to flourish in the soil of the Roman Empire in which she had been planted. It was this vision of a theocracy that provided the conceptual base for the government of what would become the Byzantine Empire. It is impossible to cover the history of Byzantine Empire in a few short pages. A summary is required, though, for

---

43   Bouyer, *Eucharist*, 64.

this was the crucible in which the Eastern Church was formed and in which it flourished. It is also an area with which very few Westerners are familiar. Two elements are important to grasp. The first is the political-historical.

The unified empire of Constantine was short lived. It operated as two halves of an integrated whole, both originally sharing the same worldview. Before the end of the fourth century the barbarian invasion of the Western part of the empire was under way, and the West was conquered in pieces. Most of the barbarians were Christianized over time, but the barbarian conquest slowed and often severely limited liturgical development in the West. The next four hundred years would see this struggle go on until the final rise of the empire of Charlemagne. The Ostrogoth kingdom was founded in Italy in 493, and most of what is now referred to as Europe was under barbarian dominion. This was the beginning of the Dark Ages in the West. In the East, the empire was not without difficulties and wars but remained essentially intact and operated as a united whole.

The barbarian invasions and conquests contributed greatly to the manner in which both the state and the Church developed in the West. With the separation of the empire into East and West, and the further disintegration of the Western empire thereafter, a political vacuum with accompanying power struggle ensued. The Church became a source of authority and often exerted itself as the authority in the world. This historical situation directly involved the Church in politics—in the world—and the Western Church, in part out of necessity and in part out of choice, elected to assert itself in this arena. The result was clericalism, what Fr. Schmemann describes as the "hierarchical subordination of the state to the church."[44] Out of this came the religious-political struggles that raged in the Dark Ages, through the period of Charlemagne into the Middle Ages, and ultimately culminated in

---

44 Schmemann, *Historical Road*, 150.

the Reformation. All this from the Church opting to operate as an entity in the world.

The second element we must grasp about Byzantium is the consequence of the first—the environment in which the Church operated. Father Schmemann contrasts what took place in the West to what occurred and developed in the East. The theocratic concept of Constantine, flawed though it was, reached its pinnacle in Justinian's reign in the sixth century. His political-religious view was *symphony*—a symbiotic relationship in which the Church and state were not connected by law nor by power, but by the Christian Faith. The emperor and the empire were bound by declaration of faith to maintain the faith in its entirety.

> In the Eastern concept, the church embraced the whole world and was its inner essence, standard and the source of its gifts of the Spirit within it, but it was not the *authority* in worldly political matters, nor even the source of authority. The latter was granted to emperors and rulers, they should be guided by the truth of the Church, but they did not receive authority from the Church.[45]

The result was that the Church was within the state and a part of it but was essentially subservient to it. In the West, the Church was within the state, often at odds with it and appearing to be outside of it, but also striving to be over it. Even with Justinian's concept of symphony, there was always the question of the arbitrary authority of the state and the Church's acceptance of it—often at its own expense and at a cost to the truth of the Kingdom of God.

Even though in the East the Church was not a power in the world, Fr. Schmemann labels both the Eastern and Western Christian experience as failures. However, the consequences of the fact that they were different are important to note. In the East

---

45 Schmemann, *Historical Road,* 118.

the empire was essentially intact for the millennium after Constantine, while the West was being divided and conquered; in the East the Church operated within this relative stability, while in the West the Church was caught in the same struggles as the state. Father Schmemann writes:

> Both East and West deviated from the Original New Testament conception of the role of the Church in relation to the state. However, the unique position of the Church within the Byzantine empire coupled with the historic circumstances of the next one thousand years created an environment which was highly enculturated, had well developed arts and sciences, yet did not fundamentally change.[46]

Father Schmemann contends that the theocracy within Byzantium cannot simply be written off as the subjugation of the Church to the state. It certainly was not the subjection of the state to the Church, which was frequently the case in the West. The relationship of Church and state was far too complex for that simplistic an assessment. Throughout its life, Byzantium experienced struggles from within: to correct moral values—as seen in the Trullan Councils; to rediscover the spiritual realities of the faith—as seen in monasticism; to define the theology of the faith—as seen in the later ecumenical councils and the work of many great theologians; to experience the fullness of Christian worship—as seen in the development of the Divine Liturgy of St. John Chrysostom. The Church was not docilely present within Byzantium as nothing more than a means of consecrating the state.

It was in this setting of relative stability and cultural development that we must see the development of the Liturgy. This culture, with its aesthetic sense and love of beauty, allowed the expression of the faith to flower. And it is worthy of note that these religious developments were not limited to forms of worship.

---

46 Schmemann, *Historical Road,* 217.

Theology in the Eastern Church continued to develop unabated and on a level equal to that in the West. And most importantly, monasticism and spirituality developed to great heights during this period. Of this Fr. Schmemann notes, "We need only open the monastic literature of these times to find a world of spirituality—such amazing refinement of the human mind, such perception and holiness, such all-embracing, wonderful concept of the final meaning of life."[47] The incorporation of all these elements into worship—art, poetry, music, and spirituality—are only natural expressions of the human spirit directed back to their Creator. It was within this cultural context that the Liturgy flowered as the human heart and spirit strove to make more beautiful and meaningful the worship of God.

The major structural change in the development of the Divine Liturgy took place by the latter part of the third century. Through this time it was not uncommon for Christian worship to still have two separate components, the synaxis (directly derived from the synagogue) and the Eucharist. The Eucharist was for believers only, and while all were expected to attend, this portion of the service was closed to nonbelievers. With the removal of persecution and the development of public worship, the need for separate services disappeared. By the end of the sixth century, holding one rite without the other had become very uncommon. The two rites had some similar and overlapping components, which were easily incorporated into each other. Prior to the synthesis, the synaxis and the Eucharist services had the following components:[48]

Synaxis or Meeting	*Eucharist*
Greeting & Response	Greeting & Response
Lections interspersed with Psalmody	Kiss of Peace
Psalmody	Offertory

---

47 Schmemann, *Historical Road,* 165.
48 Dix, *Shape of the Liturgy,* 434.

Sermon	Eucharistic Prayer
Dismissal of Catechumens	Fraction
Intercessory Prayers	Communion
Benediction	Benediction

It is very easy to see how these two services could be fused together to form two parts of one celebration. In the Eastern and Western Church this synthesis occurred and included liturgical enrichments such as the addition of hymns, expanded use of litanies, and the inclusion of the Nicene Creed. Two facts show that this synthesis was true to the original worship of the early Church. First, the synaxis is very similar to the synagogue service. Second, the Eucharist is almost identical to the Eucharist that Justin Martyr describes in his *First Apology* as taking place at Rome in AD 150.

In the context of this maturation, two points are important to keep in mind. First, as we have noted, liturgical changes of the fourth century were not a radical break with what came before. Father Schmemann says of this period, "It is really impossible to speak of a 'liturgical revolution' in the fourth century, if by this we mean the appearance of a type of worship differing radically from that which had gone before."[49] The same holds true of the enhancements and beautifications that took place in the early Byzantine period. Gregory Dix in *The Shape of the Liturgy* states that the main form of the Eastern Liturgy had been "reached by the end of the fourth century, after this the process is no more than one of adjustment and development of detail."[50]

He goes on to say that the final shape of the Liturgy was set by AD 800, with only minor variations occurring thereafter. Worth mentioning for those concerned with the lateness of this date is that most of what we take for granted as normative Christian

---

49   Schmemann, *Liturgical Theology*, 94.
50   Dix, *Shape of the Liturgy*, 546.

belief and doctrine is equally late. The authoritative formulation of the doctrines of Christ and of the Holy Trinity were also fourth-century products, the results of combating heresy. So was the formulation of the New Testament canon. The major task of the early Ecumenical Councils was defining these doctrines, the Creed, and the canon of Scripture.

What is now formally referred to as the Divine Liturgy of St. John Chrysostom was a late sixth-century finalization that took place in Constantinople. We have seen that it was in continuity with the liturgical traditions of the early Church. Prior to becoming Bishop of Constantinople, St. John had been Bishop of Antioch, and his liturgical contributions to Orthodox worship included the liturgical traditions that he brought from Antioch to Constantinople. By the seventh century the compilation of the Divine Liturgy was essentially complete, and most of the changes thereafter were not changes in substance, but rather minor changes in form and style. Minor stylistic changes took place through the ninth century, but after that only minor changes in the wording of the prayers of the Liturgy.[51]

A beautiful and moving historic verification of this fact can be seen in the Byzantine collection at Dumbarton Oaks in Washington, D.C. It is a chalice from Rhia in Byzantium, which dates from between AD 527 and 565. Inscribed around the rim are the words from the anaphora: "Thine own of Thine own we offer to Thee, O Lord"—the very words still used in the prayer before Communion today.

By the seventh century the See of Constantinople had risen to the central position in the entire Orthodox Church, and the liturgical patterns that had been synthesized in the capital began to influence other traditions. Within a short period of time the form used in the capital became the only form used within the whole Eastern Church other than on special days. The Divine Liturgy

---

51 Dix, 547.

was reaching full maturity. The time of change in response to its historical and cultural circumstance was over; the beautification and solidifying was complete. It was completely and fully expressing the meaning of the Faith and of the Eucharist, in keeping with Scripture and Tradition.

Continuity and Schism

The historical event that separated the Eastern and Western Church, the Great Schism of 1054, is one event of which most Christians are aware. However, this break in communion between the churches did not happen spontaneously; it was the result of many centuries of growing apart and of developing different worldviews.

Father Schmemann points out that "Byzantium, for its part, was increasingly turning its back on the west and shifting its center of interest eastward. From the 5th Century on, we clearly perceive the progressive orientalization of the empire and its culture, psychology, art and court ritual."[52] Although the East had been organically connected to the West from the beginning, the barbarian invasions had plunged the West deeper into the chaos of the Dark Ages. Byzantium was unable to intervene and developed in its own way, apart from the West. The political and military tensions of surviving in a hostile world, including Islam, the Slavs, and the Normans, led to the basic concern to foster religious status quo. For the Church and the empire, each religious change brought a threat of shock that the Empire could ill afford.

The reality was that by the early eighth century, the Byzantine Empire was no longer a world empire. It had become a "comparatively small state in which all was subordinated to the need of withstanding pressure: that of Islam from the east, the Slavs from

---

52 Schmemann, *Historical Road*, 143.

the north and—soon to come –the Normans from the west."[53]
From the reign of Justinian through this period, the Church had
been progressively subsumed by the state. Thus it was shaped by
the political and historical realities that determined the fate of
the empire. Both the Church and the state began to foster an attitude of isolated conservatism. That is not to say that everything
religious ceased: rather, from the tenth century onward the focus
was on the transmission of tradition and culture at the expense
of creativity. It was understood that the Catholic truth of the
Church had been formulated and compiled by the ancient Fathers
and the Ecumenical Councils, once and for all. This tendency to
look to the past, coupled with the prevailing cultural and political
worldview, resulted in the development of the notion that what
had been decided and referred to in the past was the only guarantee of Orthodoxy.

Besides providing an environment in which the Church could
naturally develop, this conservatism or absence of change is the
third major aspect of the Eastern Orthodox Church. It is one that
has great bearing on our understanding and appreciation of the
Divine Liturgy. The Church strove to be true to St. Paul's challenge to Timothy to guard the deposit of the faith (1 Tim. 6:20),
and this foundational commitment to the nature of the early
apostolic Church of Jesus Christ formed the basic view upon
which future development would occur. We have seen that the
passage of time and the need to be relevant and to fully present
the Faith resulted in a type of change—that which was true to
the Tradition of the Church and yet embodied the fullness of
the Gospel. This view was further established after the period of
the early Fathers, those bishops and theologians who described
the doctrines of belief, codified the Scriptures, and defined the
Church's worship. After this period, a certain understanding
developed that the major work had been completed, the shape

---

53 Schmemann, *Historical Road,* 200.

of the faith and practice had been established—it was a reference against which future developments would be judged. That this is still the case in varying degrees throughout Christianity can be seen in theological libraries. Often the largest section of the library of a pastor, church, or seminary will be the writings of the early Fathers. Dozens of volumes that look like legal texts—brown or tan with blue, green, or red bands—containing the writings of the ante-Nicene, Nicene, and post-Nicene Fathers, along with sets of all the other early Christian writers, testify to the foundational contribution they made. The million-dollar question is why they are so infrequently read today.

For the early Church, theology was from experience. The experience of Jesus Christ and of the Holy Spirit required the development of the doctrine of the Trinity. The experience of Jewish worship and of the Eucharist forced the development of new worship forms. By the time of the last ecumenical council, the majority of this experience had been defined. The great age of Christian theology was over: the work had been done. It was this mindset coupled to the circumstances and worldview of Byzantium that resulted in the changelessness of the Church. In spite of this, there was still "a very high level of ecclesiastical culture, spiritual and intellectual interests, and constant concern for enlightenment, schools and books. Medieval Byzantium was the cultural center of the world."[54] And in spite of this apparent contradiction (or perhaps because of it), it was here that the pinnacle of Eastern spirituality occurred, in the persons of St. Symeon the New Theologian and St. Gregory Palamas. The problem, as we look back, was that the emphasis was upon maintenance and elaboration. And while this is troublesome to us in terms of the lack of development, we must recognize something vitally important about this circumstance with regard to the Divine Liturgy.

During the last fifteen hundred years the West has undergone

---

54 Schmemann, *Historical Road*, 226.

constant change. As Alvin Toffler suggested in *The Third Wave*, change has been the constant—the variable has been the rate of change.[55] In contrast, Byzantium experienced a steady and constant period of development in its first few hundred years, and then essentially a millennium of no change. The result has been an almost unchanged reservoir of liturgical worship practice that is true to the origins of the Christian Faith. True, there were many shortcomings to Byzantium, and the Church paid a great price for being within this empire. Yet it was by no means all bad, and we have a living testament of liturgical worship as proof.

The schism of 1054, which resulted in the formal and final separation of the Western Church from the Eastern, was the result of theological, cultural, and political disputes complicated by the extreme differences between the two halves of the Christian world. The fate of Byzantium, and of the Eastern Church, had little to do with the schism of 1054. That was only one piece in the puzzle. The two had begun as two halves of an integrated whole, and Fr. Schmemann eloquently describes the result: "The fate of Byzantium was finally decided in the east, and the emergence of Islam marks the borderline that divided the early (Eastern) empire . . . from later Byzantium. The unity of the Roman world was not destroyed by an internal division between East and West, but by an external catastrophe."[56]

This external catastrophe was primarily the barbarian invasions and conquests in the West, which wrenched it from communion with the East. It was deepened by the historic and cultural process that resulted in the East being labeled "Greek" and the West "Latin," and was finally capped by the rise of Islam when the Patriarchates of Jerusalem, Alexandria, and Antioch slipped under the Islamic yoke. The remainder of the Byzantine Empire was Greek and was cut off from its brethren in the Islamic

---

55 Alvin Toffler, *The Third Wave* (New York: Bantam Books, 1981).
56 Schmemann, *Historical Road*, 150.

conquest. This disconnection, coupled with its slowly developing cultural and political differences with the West, left the Byzantine Empire isolated. Religious, cultural, and political differences, which finally resulted in schism in 1054, prevented it from looking west. Religious difference and outright hostility prevented it from looking east. Yet it could reach north—to the Slavs and to Russia. And this it did with missionary efforts that began in the ninth century.

The legacy of this missionary effort was evident in 1988 with the celebration of the millennium of Christianity in Russia—the result of this outreach northward. By the time of the fall of the Byzantine Empire in the fifteenth century, Russia was an Orthodox country, and in the view of the Russian church the holy mission of Byzantium had passed to it. This missionary effort to the Slavic countries, to Russia and on into Asia, speaks of the spiritual vitality still at work within the Eastern Church in the Byzantine Empire. The result was an Orthodox Church in Russia that undertook another millennium of worship, praise, and evangelism. Out of this missionary focus came the evangelism of Northern Asia and North America and the establishment of Orthodox Christianity in Alaska in 1793. Three of the four Orthodox saints who have been canonized in America [*as of first writing—ed.*] were Russian missionaries—Herman, Juvenaly, and Innocent—one a monk, one a priest, and the last a bishop. The fourth, an Aleut Indian named Peter, was a convert to Orthodox Christianity.

The West, meanwhile, continued to undergo dramatic change during the medieval period of Scholasticism, through the Renaissance, and on into the Enlightenment period. These changes were not only political, cultural, and philosophical, but involved substantial theological movement and innovation as well. Dix concludes the historical portion of his book with this observation:

> The Byzantine Church survived because . . . Orthodoxy is a
> far greater and more Christian thing than Byzantium—rich

in faith and holiness and above all in martyrs. Until this last twenty years it was still possible (though unfair) to call it a sleeping church. . . . It will be fascinating to see what it makes of its magnificent patristic heritage in the modern world when it has been everywhere set free from its old entanglements with autocracy. One thing it will assuredly keep is the Byzantine rite by which all Orthodoxy worships, and has saved itself from extinction by worshiping.[57]

Dix wrote this in 1943, well in advance of the current flowering of Orthodoxy, especially in America. True, Eastern Orthodox Christianity and Byzantium were separated and isolated from the West for almost a thousand years. Does this somehow mean that Orthodoxy is out of step with the times or not relevant because it hasn't changed with the times? Because it hasn't succumbed to the same cultural and social changes? Because it has held to those things that were taught and practiced from the beginning? No. Rather, it means that Western Christianity should be looking to the living liturgical legacy of Orthodox Christianity all the more.

---

57   Dix, *Shape of the Liturgy*, 548.

CHAPTER 3

Revelation and Worship

T HE ORTHODOX UNDERSTANDING OF WORSHIP begins with the conviction that there is indeed a communion of the saints in the Kingdom of God. It is not the alone worshiping the Alone. Further, this understanding affirms the scriptural premise that there are other heavenly or spiritual beings: angels and archangels, cherubim and seraphim. The Scriptures teach that in worship we are surrounded by and worship within this communion of saints and heavenly host. As the Prayer of Entrance says, "O Sovereign Lord, our God, who appointed in heaven the orders and armies of angels and archangels for the service of Your glory, grant that the holy angels may enter with us to serve and glorify Your goodness with us."

In the prayer during the Thanksgiving, we acknowledge God "for this liturgy which You are pleased to accept from our hands, though there stand before You thousands of archangels, and myriads of angels, cherubim and seraphim, six-winged, many-eyed, soaring high on their wings; singing, proclaiming, shouting the hymn of victory." Our worship involves this heavenly host, as revealed for instance in Isaiah 6:1–8, because our worship takes place in the Kingdom of God, before the heavenly throne.

We pray for those who partake of the gifts of the Eucharist:

Furthermore, we offer to You this spiritual worship for those who in faith have gone on before us to their rest: forefathers, fathers, patriarchs, prophets, apostles, preachers, evangelists, martyrs, confessors, ascetics, and every righteous spirit made perfect in faith, especially for our most holy, most pure, most blessed and glorious Lady, the Mother of God and Ever-Virgin Mary.

Unlike us moderns, Christians through the ages have affirmed the "great cloud of witnesses" (Heb. 12:1), those saints who have gone before us, and pray for them even as we believe and expect that they pray for us.

When we gather to worship, especially to celebrate the Divine Liturgy, we recognize that it is not just those of us on earth who are present, but those gathered as "the general assembly and church of the firstborn *who are* registered in heaven" (Heb. 12:23). These saints are simply those among all Christians who have led particularly spiritual or exemplary lives in Christ. The Church has recognized this and held them up as especially worthy of honor by those of us striving to be conformed to the image of Christ. We who as Christians pray and are prayed for usually give hardly a thought to the prospect of asking a brother or sister to pray for us in times of trouble or need. Inasmuch as the saints departed this life have gone to be with the Lord and are alive in the Kingdom, then is it at all unusual to ask for their prayers on our behalf? They are saints who share the same spiritual communion as we do; they constitute the communion of the saints. Thus it is no different to ask intercession or prayer of them than it is to ask intercession or prayer of one another.

For the Christian, death is not the end, nor is it an eternal holding pattern. Rather, life continues in the Kingdom of God, as St. Paul declares: "to be absent from the body [is] to be at home with the Lord" (2 Cor. 5:8). If we indeed believe that life continues spiritually after the physical death, then we should have little trouble affirming this understanding of the saints. Taken one step further, if any of us are undergoing trial and tribulation then to some extent our salvation is in jeopardy; thus, to ask a brother or sister to pray for us is to ask them to pray for our salvation. This is exactly what is intended when, during the Liturgy, this petition is offered up to God: "Through the prayers of the Mother of God, O Savior, save us."

One of the more striking and unusual elements of the Divine Liturgy for Protestants is prayer to the Mother of God, the Theotokos. Contrary to popular Protestant belief, this prayer does not constitute idolatry or worship of the Virgin Mary. For she is the God-bearer, the Mother of God, she who bore Jesus Christ, who is God incarnate. The term *Theotokos* is not an Orthodox aberration; rather, it was the term decided upon by the synod of Ephesus in AD 431, during the Nestorian controversy, as that which most correctly described Mary and protected the proper Christological understanding of Jesus as the Messiah of God. Two great doctrines came out of this council: the first, the Incarnation, is still affirmed by most Christians; the second, understanding Mary as Theotokos, is only fully retained by the Orthodox Church.

The doctrinal decision of the council about the Incarnation— that Jesus Christ was fully human *and* fully divine—is near and dear to the hearts of Christians. In the process the term *Theotokos* was introduced to ensure this understanding: the word means "God-bearer" and clearly states that the One Mary bore was God. As the council determined, the two understandings go hand in hand: we cannot take one without the other and still be true to early Christianity. Had God Himself not been in her womb, we would be doomed. As Fr. Thomas Hopko points out, "Jesus Christ, the Son, Word, and image of God, is physically and spiritually formed in the body of Mary so that He might be formed in us as well (see Gal. 4:19)."[58]

---

58 Thomas Hopko, *The Winter Pascha* (Crestwood, NY: St. Vladimir's

This role of honor is most clearly seen in the final petition in the litanies: "Remembering our most holy, most pure, most blessed, most glorious Lady, the Mother of God and Ever-Virgin Mary, with all the saints, let us commit ourselves and each other and all our lives unto Christ our God." Look closely at the wording. We say, "Remembering Mary . . . we *commit* ourselves to Christ."

What is meant here? Simply that we hold up Mary as the first person to receive Christ, the one human being whose life was most fully in conformity with the will of God. In this modern society, where unmarried mothers are an everyday occurrence, we hardly consider the familial, social, and religious cost to Mary for having cooperated with the will of God for her life. She is a study in humility and submission to the will of God. That is how we must live also. In remembering Mary's life, in calling her "blessed" as the New Testament teaches, we recommit each day to live in conformity to Christ in the image and will of God.

The saints, because of the lives they lived, become icons or images—models—of what the Christian life should be: humble, loving, and spiritual. Thus they provide us with real and tangible models to which we should strive to conform our own lives. Most of the early saints were martyrs, those who willingly died for their belief in Jesus Christ. This was a testimony not only to the faith of the individual who was martyred, but because of their willingness to die for their Lord, it was also a testimony to the triumph of Christ over death. That is why so many early churches were built with their altars over the grave of a martyr: the martyr's death was a testimony to the Resurrection of Jesus Christ, as the Eucharist offered on that altar was spiritual food providing us eternal life. The saints may have died physically, but we who believe know that they have not died in any final sense; they live on with Christ in His Kingdom. If life after death is part of our

Seminary Press, 1984), 22.

Christian belief, then what we affirm is the reality of the communion of the saints.

Is the belief in the communion of the saints as a present reality a medieval or modern innovation? No: it goes back to the early Church. Saint Athanasius speaks of it in AD 330, in his second pastoral letter regarding the Easter feast, and this undoubtedly reflects a much earlier tradition within the Church. Remember, this is the same St. Athanasius who defended the divinity of Christ and drew up the first list of canonical books that became the New Testament. He says, "So then, let us celebrate this heavenly joy, together with the saints of old who kept the same Feast. Yes, they keep the feast with us, and they are examples to us of life in Christ."[59] Notice the change in tenses: the saints of old kept, and now they keep it with us. The saints are able to keep the feast because upon their death they entered into the communion of the Lord that transcends death and is eternal.

This understanding of the saints as models, as images of the Christian life and thus of Christ, helps us understand the Orthodox use of icons. The icons are images, models or visual aids by which we can visualize these persons whom we venerate. But why icons? For the same reason we have pictures of loved ones around the house or in our wallets. We are human beings, strongly shaped and controlled by our senses. Further, our Faith is a concrete one rooted in history and experience and centered in a flesh-and-blood Savior who is God. In Hebrews 12, Christians are seen as "looking unto Jesus." Thus the use of icons becomes quite practically important.

The Scriptures teach that we were created by God as physical as well as spiritual beings. To deny this physical aspect of our being is in fact to deny the nature of the creation. The challenge is to

---

59 Jack Sparks, ed., *The Resurrection Letters: An Early Church Leader Reflects on Easter* (Nashville, TN: Thomas Nelson Publishers, 1979), 60.

affirm this physical aspect of our being in a manner that is edifying and that builds us up and conforms us to the image of Christ. Furthermore, the Incarnation of Jesus, the taking on of human flesh and possessing both human and divine natures, is the ultimate affirmation of the inherent goodness of creation. We were created as physical and spiritual beings, and we are being saved as such. To deny the physical side of our being, or to affirm the spiritual at the expense of the physical, is simply not Christian. In worship all of our senses are involved. We smell the incense, and for those of us familiar with its use in worship, it not only symbolizes prayers rising to God (Ps. 140/141:2); its very smell, with all of its associations, creates an atmosphere of worship. We hear, we touch, we see, and we taste—all in a celebration that elevates us above routine physical existence to realize we are seated in the heavenly realms in Christ Jesus.

Anyone who seriously attempts to pray or to meditate knows that just as soon as the eyes close and prayer begins, so does the struggle. The mind is immediately filled with a million and one thoughts and distractions. Prayer is a constant battle. That is why the atmosphere or ambience of worship is so important; it should be different from our normal and harried lifestyle; it should be of a nature to facilitate our moving into prayer and worship. This is one of the reasons why Orthodox Christians often carry icons with them in their travel, and have icons in their homes. In the midst of a busy schedule, pressing engagements, and all the rest of it, it is difficult to make the time to pray, let alone to be able to focus when praying. It is amazing and wonderful how the presence of these simple and small icons facilitates praying. They help direct our efforts and keep us focused on the work at hand.

Ernst Benz is a Protestant theologian who writes to explain Orthodox Christianity. He contends that the Orthodox Church cannot be fully understood until one understands its icons.[60] This

---

60   Ernst Benz, *The Eastern Orthodox Church: Its Thought and Life*

begins in seeing the relationship between God and humankind, for humans were created in the image of God and carry this icon of God within themselves. Benz believes that "this image-concept also dominates the Christology and doctrine of the Trinity in the Eastern Church."[61] Christ, the divine Word, is the image of the Father. The redemptive work of Jesus Christ, who is the icon of the Father, consists in renewing the image of God that was distorted by sin. Redemption is linked to this concept of image; the redemption of mankind "consists in mankind's being renewed in the image of Jesus Christ, incorporated into the new image of Christ, and thus through Jesus Christ experiencing the renewal of his status as image of God."[62]

At the heart of all iconography is Jesus Christ, and thus God the Father. The saint portrayed in an icon is in the image of Jesus Christ. In venerating the saints, we are in fact venerating Jesus Christ ("He who receives you receives Me" [Matt. 10:40]); that is, they will receive God, in whose image and likeness they were made. Icons serve to challenge and motivate us, to encourage and bless us—because in them we see and experience Jesus Christ, the hope of glory.

As we've seen with the first-century synagogue at Migdal, the stone box found in that archaeological excavation was decorated with carvings—specific symbolism that connected it to the temple in Jerusalem. Older Jewish synagogues frequently contained illustrations of biblical scenes, symbols, or stories—until the third or fourth century, when in anti-Christian reaction the use of all such imagery was proclaimed idolatrous. In fact, archaeological excavations have shown great similarity between the frescoes and mosaics used in some synagogues and those used in early Christian iconography. The excavations of both a synagogue and

---

(New York: Anchor Books, 1963), 18.

61   Benz, *The Eastern Orthodox Church*, 19.

62   Benz, 19.

a Christian church in Dura-Europos, on the Euphrates in what is now Syria, testify to this fact.[63] These particular buildings date to approximately AD 265 and confirm the common iconography in synagogue and church. This might be parallel development, but it could just as easily be a natural progression. The older Jewish stories are now interpreted in the light of Christ. It was the rampant martyrdom of believers that initiated the painting of icons of particular saints; their icons bore witness to the eternal life that was theirs in Christ and that their death proclaimed.

In the first millennium of the Church, when the majority of the populace was illiterate, the icons functioned as books for the people. More recently they have been called "the gospel in color." They provided images, with the associated facts and history, of those who had gone before in the faith.

In fact, icons keep us from idolatry. An icon of Christ, for example, keeps us from creating or making up our own versions of Jesus. Recall that the Ecumenical Councils were held to determine once and for all the nature of Jesus Christ. Icons, by definition, are very stylized and are not naturalistic. They are not supposed to represent the scene or person as if in a portrait or photograph. They are for spiritual and prayerful purposes, and the veneration given them is referred to the person represented, and thus ultimately to Christ, not to the image.

By keeping iconography stylized and structured, the Church has attempted to minimize our tendency to imagine things as they suit us. Icons of the Incarnation or of the Resurrection, for instance, are filled with images that not only illustrate the occurrence, but also convey the full meaning of what took place. I had the pleasure recently to see an exhibit of thirteenth- and fourteenth-century Greek-Byzantine icons in a collection touring America. It was glorious; the work was spectacular. It was

---

63   Jean Lassus, *The Early Christian and Byzantine World* (New York: McGraw-Hill, 1967), 17.

also troublesome, though, to be viewing them in a gallery as art, rather than being before them prayerfully in church, where they would move us beyond the here and now to Christ and His Kingdom. All of us as humans tend to try to take God on our own terms. Icons force us to continually accept, worship, and believe in Jesus Christ, and to do so as the Church has taught from the beginning.

Iconography and the Incarnation go hand in hand. In Jesus Christ dwells the fullness of the Godhead, and although no one has seen God, yet Christ reveals Him in full; therefore, an image of Jesus Christ is an image of God. If the purpose of the Incarnation was to redeem fallen creation, then all matter has the capability of being sanctified by the grace of the Holy Spirit. Thus, a portrayal of Christ is not only an image but may become a spiritual reality. This is simply because, as a result of the Incarnation, everything has taken on new meaning.

As we will see in Part II, one of the first things to strike us upon entering an Orthodox Church is the icon screen, or iconostasis. It is at the front of the church, before the altar, and is composed of a variety of icons. It is there not only to decorate the Church: at the very least it is there to help us enter into prayer and worship by calling to mind those represented. As we will see in Chapter 5, it evokes the ascent to the Kingdom, for we enter in with Christ and the saints, who are here represented. Even if at the very least it is only a projection in painting or mosaic of the vision of the Church assembled together for worship, it is "the most successful attempt, maybe, in the whole history of the Christian Church, to make the invisible visible in Christian worship."[64]

A favorite phrase of St. Paul is "image of Christ." We all pray for, preach, and teach that we should be conformed to the image of Christ. In so doing, what are we asking for? That we might be more like Him. And the Greek word translated as "image" is *icon*.

---

64 Bouyer, *Eucharist*, 70.

CHAPTER 4

The Royal Priesthood

I N SAYING THAT THE COMMUNION of saints is at the heart of Orthodox worship, we must next turn to see how that worship or liturgy is celebrated. More than celebrated, it is co-celebrated by the clergy and the people gathered to praise the one true God. But it is also co-celebrated with the saints and the heavenly host, for we are all saints together, equally children of God brought into the Kingdom by the sacrifice of Jesus Christ through the work of the Holy Spirit. It is this communion that forms the basis of our worship: we join with those in heaven before the Throne of God and offer Him praise and blessing.

Those who have been reconciled to God through belief in Jesus Christ in holy baptism become members of the royal priesthood. This priesthood, commonly referred to as the priesthood of believers (see 1 Pet. 2:9), is foundational to Christianity.

What is a priest? One who stands before God and offers to Him in thanksgiving that which He has given to us: life. Because of the Fall, humanity turned away from the worship of God and became self-centered. In the Letter to the Romans, St. Paul isolates the key mark of sin: unthankfulness (1:21). Man refuses to say thank you to God, to love Him back. But as reconciled believers, we are "a chosen generation, a royal priesthood, a holy nation" (1 Pet. 2:9–10); we are now the people of God. Having been restored to our priesthood, we come back to worship. Father Schmemann writes:

> All rational, spiritual and other qualities of man distinguishing him from other creatures have their focus and ultimate fulfillment in this capacity to bless God, to know, so to speak, the meaning of the thirst and hunger that constitute his life. 'Homo Sapien,' 'Homo Faber,' . . . yes, but first of all, 'Homo adorans'. The first, the basic definition of man is that he is the priest. He stands in the center of the world and unifies it in his act of blessing God, of both receiving the world from God and offering it to God—and by filling the world with this Eucharist, he transforms his life, the one that he receives from the world, into life in God, into communion with Him.[65]

And at the most practical level, what does this mean for us? It means that we were created to bless and praise God, to worship Him. This is our vocation. Vocation, you say, as in work? Yes! Vocation, because this is precisely what we were created to do, to be in communion with God as His priests, and in that role to worship Him. The dictionary defines *vocation* as follows: "any occupation or pursuit for which one qualifies oneself, or to which one devotes one's time or life; a calling."[66] We are not only called to this way of life, we were created for it. And in accepting Jesus Christ as Lord and Savior and entering into the Church, we are enabled by God's Holy Spirit to carry out that for which we were created. As we have seen, *liturgy* literally means "the work of the people." This work is not just what we are to do during the Divine Liturgy but that work that we are to do throughout all of our lives.

---

65 Schmemann, *For the Life of the World*, 15.
66 *Funk & Wagnalls New Standard Dictionary of the English Language* (1913), s.v. "vocation."

There is a personal issue to be considered here, however, and it has to do with the fulfillment of this fundamental attribute for which we were created. The inherent ability to be a priest may be exercised to varying degrees or not at all. Those who are outside the New Covenant of faith in Jesus Christ and are not members of His Body are not fulfilling this created purpose. They possess the capacity, by having been created in the image of God, but they are not able to actualize it until they are reconciled to God in Jesus Christ. Those within the New Covenant have been restored to this priesthood, and for them the question of fulfillment becomes the issue.

It must be said that the understanding of humans as priests is but one aspect of their role in creation. In theology Christ is understood to have manifested Himself in three offices: as King, High Priest, and Prophet. Christ is King because He is the anointed Messiah; He is Priest because He offered Himself for the life of the world; He is Prophet because He fulfilled all the prophecies in coming in human form. Notice that all three are connected to the human nature that Jesus Christ took upon Himself in the Incarnation. It was through taking on and fulfilling His calling in human form that He became King, High Priest, and Prophet. These three offices or characteristics of Christ are also the created offices or characteristics of human beings. We were created to be priestly, prophetic and kingly; and though fallen, this is what we can become in Jesus Christ.

St. Paul observed that "all things work together for good to those who love God, to those who are the called according to *His* purpose" (Rom. 8:28), indicating a fundamental interrelationship of all we are and do in Jesus Christ. This is equally true of the Church. The liturgical and the sacramental aspects of the Church are linked together, and as we have seen, they are the way the Church is to be and to worship. This was so from the beginning of the New Testament Church. Our ability to fulfill this vocation, this calling, as priest is directly tied to the liturgical and the sacramental. Until we accept and put on these characteristics of the Church, we will be members of the royal priesthood, but we will never fulfill our calling as priests.

It is this priesthood that undergirds Christian worship, most particularly the Divine Liturgy. Why? Because our worship can and must take place in the only place of true worship, the Kingdom of God. The Liturgy is a celebration of our salvation. It is a feast of the joy that is ours in the Holy Trinity, which Christ came to give. It is saying thank you for the grace of God, which is continually available to us through the Holy Spirit in the sacraments. It is a festival with all the accompanying joy and gladness that characterize heaven itself.

Jesus described the Kingdom of God in terms of a royal feast: "They will come from the east and the west, from the north and the south, and sit down in the kingdom of God" (Luke 13:29). And St. John tells us in Revelation that the saints at the heavenly wedding feast cry out, "Alleluia! For the Lord God Omnipotent reigns! Let us be glad and rejoice and give Him glory, for the marriage of the Lamb has come, and His wife has made herself ready" (Rev. 19:6–7).

This explains why at the beginning of the eucharistic meal in Acts, Luke writes that "they ate their food with gladness and simplicity of heart" (Acts 2:46). Our hearts are to be filled with joy as we experience communion with our risen Lord. As Benz points out, "The Orthodox liturgy has preserved unchanged this early Christian mood of rejoicing and spiritual gladness. In this its character is quite different from the Eucharist in, say, Reformed Christianity, where the early Christian spirit of gladness is clouded and obscured by the spirit of penitence."[67]

---

67 Benz, *Eastern Orthodox Church*, 23.

The Priesthood in Action: Worship

In worship, celebration takes two forms: concelebration and co-celebration. *Concelebration* is a term used to describe how priests and deacons celebrate together their part of the Liturgy. Co-celebration describes the role the clergy take in the Liturgy with the congregation. We all celebrate together, or co-celebrate, this worship that is offered up to the Holy Trinity and is called the Divine Liturgy. The sacramental role that the priest performs is done on behalf of the gathered believers; the priest and the assembly of believers offer their worship to God as a corporate whole. The priest leads the assembly in their corporate worship, as Christ leads the mystical Body as its Head. The royal priesthood of all believers—both clergy and laity—assures each of God's people access to Him and makes this worship possible.

Archbishop Philip Saliba stated it as poignantly as possible in an address to Orthodox clergy:

> The Church started as a worshiping community. Even during the era of persecution, the Church never failed to come together for worship and the celebration of the Eucharist. Notice that I did not use the term "to perform" the Divine Liturgy: because the early Christians did not "act" the liturgy; they celebrated it. To celebrate an event is to observe it in a very special way. The priests and the congregation are the celebrators while Christ is the celebrity *par excellence*. To celebrate the Eucharist is to encounter Christ.[68]

The priest has a specific sacramental role; he is called to the priesthood as the father of the faithful ordained by the bishop, and that role includes leading the worship, preaching, and consecrating

---

68   Philip Saliba, *Feed My Sheep* (Crestwood, NY: St. Vladimir's Seminary Press, 1987), 43.

and serving the Eucharist. The priest is first and foremost the icon of Christ to His people, and the designation "father" connotes the pastoral role he is to have. He is president of the holy assembly, the man who stands in front representing the bishop and bringing the entire priesthood to the throne of God. Recall that in the early Church, the bishop was the central figure around whom the congregation gathered to celebrate the Eucharist. The bishop, as direct successor to the apostles, was the representative, the icon of Christ. And so the priest, as the representative of the bishop, is the icon of Christ to His people.

The key role of the bishop in maintaining the integrity and continuity of what Christ began was not a late political or medieval development, designed to further the power of the Church within the state. For Eusebius, apostolic succession was a crucial and critical issue. It is not only apparent doctrinally: if we consider the structure of his treatise *The History of The Church*, we see that it is linked together like a chain. And what constitutes the links? The bishops of each church. His entire history from the time of Christ through the ascent of Constantine is traced *from bishop to bishop*.

For Eusebius, apostolic succession is critical because "that succession includes the whole intellectual, spiritual, and institutional life of the Church, and is the guarantee of the preservation of one unchanging God-given doctrine."[69] He quotes Philo, the Jewish historian, who "writes about the comparative status of those entrusted with the ministries of the Church, from the diaconate to the highest and most important office, the episcopate."[70]

What makes the Church fully itself is the presence of the Lord. As the icon of Christ, the priest invokes the sacramental presence of the Lord. In Hebrew the word *qahal* means "to congregate," "to be gathered together in the presence of the Lord," or

---

69 Eusebius, *History of the Church*, 21.
70 Eusebius, 93.

"the gathering where the Lord is present." The important element here is that *the Lord is present,* that He is doing the gathering, and that we have assembled in response to and in anticipation of His action among us. True, we all share the royal priesthood, but sacramentally the Church needs the priest to be the Church. This understanding of the assembly gathered together by the Lord, where He is present to act, can be seen in Exodus 35:1, Deuteronomy 4:10 and 5:22, 1 Chronicles 20:14, and numerous other Old Testament references, and this understanding carries through into the New Testament.

It is worth noting at this juncture that the frequently quoted passage from Matthew 18:20, "where two or three are gathered together in My name, I am there in the midst of them," is not a stand-alone proposition. It has a very specific context, and that context is the Church. The whole teaching begins at verse 15, where Christ instructs that if our brother sins against us, we should go to him privately; failing that, take witnesses; and "if he refuses to hear them, tell *it* to the *Church*." The Lord then goes on to say that whatever you bind on earth will be bound in heaven, and that when "two of you agree on earth concerning anything that they ask, it will be done for them by My Father in heaven."

The context throughout is the Church and church discipline. It is not just any two or three people, believers or not, deciding on something. Christ's own word was *Church*. And what keeps the Church being the Church is the apostolic succession: the sacramental role of the priest as the delegate of the bishop and the continuity from bishop to bishop back to Christ.

While we have acknowledged that the priest in his sacramental role as the icon of Christ is necessary for the celebration of the Eucharist, we must realize that more than the priest is necessary. For the Orthodox Church, it has always been understood that three elements must be present together: people, priest, and the Holy Spirit. This is apparent in the prayer of consecration, in which he prays, "Send down Thy Holy Spirit upon us and upon these Gifts," and the people respond, "Amen." Then in the next two prayers: "And make this bread the precious Body of thy Christ, and that which is in this cup the precious Blood of thy Christ," to which the people again respond, "Amen." Finally, in response to the final prayer, "changing them by your Holy Spirit," the people declare, "Amen, Amen, Amen."

The Liturgy is the work of the people, and people and priest are required; a priest cannot celebrate the Eucharist without the people present. The mystical work whereby the elements become the Body and Blood require the prayers and presence of the priest and the people and the work of the Holy Spirit. Christ is present and works through His icon, the priest; the people of God are exercising their royal priesthood; the Holy Spirit mystically works in their midst, making the gifts the Body and Blood.

In fact, St. Paul understands himself as possessing this priesthood. In Romans 15:16 he says that he is a "minister of Jesus Christ to the Gentiles, ministering the gospel of God." The two words that are translated as *minister* in this sentence in most English translations are not the same. The second is the word *hierourgos*, which shares the same root word with our word *hierarch*. It is accurately translated as "to serve as a priest," not as "to administer." The same word is used by Clement of Rome in AD 95–96 to mean *priesthood*, "a special reality not possessed by those who have not received it by transmission from the Apostles as their successors."[71] This view of himself as priest is again apparent in 1 Corinthians 10:16, where St. Paul says "the cup of blessing which we bless." This refers to the liturgical prayer of consecration that is still said by the priest in every Divine Liturgy.

This has been the conviction of the Church from the beginning, and we can still see this expectation of the presence and action of the Lord within His Body in the proclamation of the

---

71 Johanny, *Eucharist of the Early Christians,* 30.

deacon before the Divine Liturgy begins. The deacon declares to the priest, "It is time for the Lord to act!" This is a clear anticipation that the Lord through the Holy Spirit will be in our midst and will be so sacramentally through the priest, His icon. This sacramental role of the priest does not reduce the value of each believer, for all of us are to be icons of Christ, because we are all made in His image (Genesis 1 and 5). Rather, it is exactly this royal priesthood that allows and enables us to come together—to be present when and where the Lord acts, and to work with Him in this responsibility called worship.

But, many might say, does not liturgical worship by its very design and structure create a distinction between clergy and laity? Yes, in an outward or organizational sense—but not in terms of standing before God. Two observations here may expand our understanding of these apparent distinctions. We have attempted in this book to show that Eastern Christianity has remained true to the practices common to all of Christianity from the beginning. One of these practices is standing during worship, which is still practiced in Orthodox Churches and was practiced in Western Christianity through the seventeenth century. In Orthodox churches in the Old World, there are no pews, only seats on the sides or at the rear for the aged and infirm. This was indeed the practice in Jewish synagogues and in the earliest Christian churches, where we saw that the assembly gathered around the bema and then moved to the altar.

The historic worship practice has been that of standing most of the time, kneeling for short periods, but never sitting. Listen to Fr. Bouyer's observation on this practice:

> In the view of the modern Western Christian this may seem an intolerable burden. But when one has become accustomed to the practice it is impossible not to realize how much of the feeling of intense participation always felt in an Orthodox liturgy is due to it. A seated assembly is

necessarily a passive assembly. And it is not disposed by its position to worship, but at best to accept some instruction, or most of the time just to look more or less curiously at a spectacle in which it takes no part. Even when it kneels to pray it will be for a private prayer and not for a common supplication. And just as a sitting assembly usually sings badly or not at all, it is hopeless to try to bring it together to praise and thanksgiving.[72]

This brings us to the matter of music in worship. Historically, liturgical services have by definition been *sung* services. The clergy and people perform the work of worship and the text is either chanted or sung by the celebrant or antiphonally between him and the congregation. Without a liturgical theology and liturgical structure, music becomes an aesthetic or emotional experience with a religious text.

The earliest form of Christian singing was psalmody received directly from Judaism. Over time more complicated music forms developed to expand and beautify the Church's worship. Originally, as the Church spread across the Greek-speaking Roman Empire, what was adopted was classical Greek forms of modal singing. Over time these developed into the larger category of liturgical chant we now refer to as Byzantine chant, concentrated in the eastern part of the Empire. In Rome and the surrounding areas, Old Roman chant developed, which in time became Gregorian chant. As there were multiple cultural expressions in the Church and as worship took place in the vernacular (local) language, it is not surprising that multiple forms of church music developed, each based on those local cultural traditions.

For the Protestant there are far fewer liturgical similarities because of the tendency of the leaders of the Reformation to discard all Roman Catholic liturgy and practice. The Protestant may

---

72 Bouyer, *Eucharist*, 97.

be familiar with the use of litanies, the Scripture readings, the sermon, and perhaps some of the intercessory prayers, but these components are only the remnants of the early Church's original order of worship.

What has been removed over time, in addition to regular Communion, are the antiphonal litanies, most of the eucharistic prayers, and other liturgical elements that are the very things that make the Divine Liturgy what it is: an interactive celebration. Protestantism uses the term *royal priesthood* more frequently than do either the Orthodox or the Roman Churches—the result of Reformation theology. Yet what does Protestantism mean by the term other than direct access to God without a mediator? It certainly suggests little or no sacramentality, for throughout most of Protestantism the Eucharist is understood as a remembrance— not as a sacrament. By extension then, the minister has no sacramental role to exercise, and neither do the people. So then, the people are not fulfilling their created role to be liturgical: they are not involved in the work of worship. With both the sacramental and the liturgical gone, the Protestant understanding of the royal priesthood has been robbed of most of its substance.

Thus, in both the Roman Catholic and Protestant services, there is a high degree to which almost all of the service is done or performed for the worshiper. One *attends* church or *goes* to Mass: the congregational role is observational. Aside from some collective singing of hymns, a confession of sin, and the recitation of the Lord's Prayer or a creed, one witnesses the act of worship taking place. It should be said that Orthodox Christians are just as susceptible to falling into this mindset. However, as we have come to understand the Divine Liturgy and the worship of the Orthodox Church, we see that the structure and form that have been preserved from the beginning truly work to involve all present in worship.

Our choice of terms often illustrates an underlying belief

system. Indeed, some even call the sanctuary the *auditorium*, the place of listening. Frequently what is going on is an interaction between performer and audience. And much professional seminary training emphasizes the sermon as the critical element of the worship experience. Its preparation becomes the most important part of a good minister's week. The emphasis on exegesis, public speaking, preaching, and application, via the three-point sermon format, have put an often-unbearable load on the minister to produce and perform.

Further, for many Protestants, with Communion typically occurring only once a month or once a quarter, there is little sense of the sacramental experience, a building toward the celebration of the Eucharist. This is a radical departure from the early Christian Church. As R. A. Torrey asserted years ago, worship is the missing jewel in Protestantism.

From the very opening of the Liturgy, what is apparent in Orthodox worship is the interactive dynamic we have referred to as co-celebration. The priest offers a prayer of blessing to God, and the congregation responds in confirmation of this offering and in lifting it heavenward. Throughout the Liturgy the congregation is directly involved in the activity of worship, actualizing its privilege and responsibility as a priesthood to worship the Holy Trinity.

It is this understanding of the communion of the saints participating in the Eucharist—made possible by the royal priesthood of believers—that makes the Divine Liturgy the dynamic, joyous, and beautiful experience it is. It is the oneness we share before God as a priesthood restored to its original purpose that allows us to fulfill our calling and offer up praise and worship to the Lord. It is, in fact, our original nature—created in the image of God—that is acknowledged each time the priest censes the congregation. Incense is employed not just to make the sanctuary smell good: it is symbolic of our prayers rising up to God (Ps.

140/141:2) and is offered as a blessing to Him who alone is our sanctification.

This act of censing, then, pays tribute to the image of God in each believer and to our restored ability to offer up worship to God. The reality of the communion of the saints is responsible, at least in part, for the dynamic and transcendent nature of the Divine Liturgy. It is not only the co-celebration of clergy and people but also their co-celebration with the saints and the host of heaven before the throne of God that sets this worship apart as more than just the people gathered together at a given time in a given place. All of earth joins all of heaven to worship together in the Kingdom of God. And as we shall see in the following pages, it is the Kingdom of God to which we ascend. For it is there that all true and spiritual worship takes place.

CHAPTER 5

Heavenly Worship

W ORSHIP BEGINS IN HEAVEN. THE Holy Scriptures record numerous instances of the drama of heavenly adoration taking place before the very throne of God. It may be that for the person familiar with Scripture some of these are so apparent that they are overlooked.

The concept of heavenly worship begins, as we have seen, with God's revelation to the children of Israel about the building of the tabernacle and the manner of worship to take place within it. This revelation formed the basis for the Old Testament worship of the Jews. Worship on earth was to reflect worship in heaven.

Other instances of heavenly worship fill out our understanding. For example, in Isaiah 6 the prophet writes of being caught up to heaven and experiencing celestial worship. He tells us there were seraphim praising God, singing "Holy, holy, holy *is* the Lord of Hosts; the whole earth *is* full of His glory" (verse 3). He records that one of the seraphim flew to him with a coal taken from the altar and touched his mouth, taking away his sin—and this was understood by the early Fathers as being a type (or model) of the Eucharist. It was after this experience that Isaiah was commissioned by God to prophesy to His people. He ties this transporting vision into earthly time: the year King Uzziah died, about 731 BC (Is. 6:1). Even the Prophet Daniel reports that his vision was from being before the throne of the Ancient of Days, where He was served and ministered to (7:9–14).

The temple in Jerusalem was the center of Jewish worship, and its center was the Holy of Holies. We've seen that the stone box excavated in the first-century Migdal synagogue in Galilee was decorated with symbolism representing the temple, and in addition to the temple menorah, the back panel with the wheels and fire represented the Holy of Holies—in other words, it represented the place in the temple where God or the Spirit of God was believed to reside. Further, in Revelation 4 and 5 the Apostle John was likewise caught up to heaven, and in that book we have the revelation of what he saw and of what he was told. He witnessed worship before the throne of God. He records the presence of twenty-four elders before the throne bowing down before the Lord. Angelic creatures are praising God, saying, "Holy, holy, holy, Lord God Almighty, who was and is and is to come!" (4:8). In fact, he sees tens of thousands of angels worshiping the Lamb who was slain (5:11–12), and "every creature which is in heaven and on the earth and under the earth and such as are in the sea, and all that are in them" worshiping the Lamb (5:13). Talk about heavenly Liturgy!

The inescapable context in all of these accounts is that of worship: worship of God by all of His creatures. And it is with this basic understanding that Orthodoxy approaches worship: it is the privilege and the responsibility of each person to bless God, that is, to praise and give thanks to the Holy Trinity for mercy and creation. We have to decide to agree with and accept the witness of Scripture or not. And whether or not we agree or fully understand it, the Bible testifies that there is worship in heaven.

By extension then, it is only natural that our worship should be in keeping with the nature of worship in heaven. The constant struggle both in Israel and in Christendom has been to avoid affirming the methods that mankind proposes as the means to approach and worship God, and instead to accept that revelation that God Himself has given us and to act on it. That is true theologically, and it is true liturgically as well. Our worship is based on revelation. The early Christian Church used the Old Testament revelation as its starting point and fulfilled it with the new and final revelation in Jesus Christ.

The summary New Testament passage on heavenly worship is Hebrews 8:1–6. Here Jesus Christ is described as our High Priest, seated at the right hand of God, who has accomplished our salvation and reconciliation through His mediation. Verse 2 tells us that this High Priest has another role also. He is the liturgist (the word is *leitourgos,* as we have seen) of the sanctuary. Jesus Christ Himself is liturgist, and this Liturgy takes place in the true tabernacle which is in heaven before the throne of God. Verses 4 and 5 tell us that worship on earth is patterned after that in heaven. This, we learn in verse 6, is the "more excellent ministry" that He has obtained because He is the Mediator of "a better covenant." The teaching is quite clear—liturgical worship is not optional. Rather, it is normative for Christians.

Worship on earth, then, is to be an extension, a reflection, of worship in the Kingdom. It is to be a window to heaven. Far be it from us to decide that this or that is unnecessary and disposable because it is not contemporary or in vogue. Our obligation is to follow and to serve God, to accept His revelation. This is the guardianship of Tradition in the life of the Church: to remain true to the faith as revealed, as it was in the beginning.

Recall in the Book of Acts when the followers of the Way were first called Christians, meaning those who followed or acted like Jesus Christ. The implication is clear. *The believers* were living lives that resembled the very life that Christ lived. So are we to live: conformed to the will of God, loving and caring for our brothers and sisters. And so are we to worship: in a heavenly pattern that shows forth the Kingdom of God in which Jesus Christ reigns.

The Kingdom of God is the critical element of worship for good reason. It was the reality and advent of this Kingdom that constituted the core of the preaching and teaching of Jesus, especially in His parables.

From the New Testament we can make three summary observations about the nature of the Kingdom of God. First, it is a present *spiritual reality* (Rom. 14:17), as well as the realm or dimension into which followers of Jesus have entered (Col. 1:13). Second, it is the *reign* or *rule of God* that has been established in Jesus Christ and will be consummated when He returns (Matt. 8:11, 11:27). Third, it is the *future inheritance* that will be bestowed upon God's people when Christ comes in glory (Matt. 25:34).

The Kingdom of God is here, but there. It has come, but has yet to come. Christ came to bring us into the Kingdom of His Father. This is where our focus must be. Father Thomas Hopko describes it well when he says:

> The two comings of Christ are held together in Christian thought, action, and prayer at all times. They cannot be separated. When they are, it is the end of the Christian faith, life and worship. The first coming without the second is a meaningless tragedy. The second coming without the first is an absurd impossibility. Jesus is born to bring God's Kingdom. He dies to prove His kingship. He rises to establish His reign. He comes again in glory to share it with His people. In the Kingdom of God there are no subjects. All rule with the risen Messiah. He came, and is coming, for this purpose alone.[73]

We, as believers in Jesus Christ, live both in this world and in the Kingdom of God. We experience the Kingdom in our midst through the work of the Holy Spirit. Based upon our faith, we know it is the eternal life we have begun to experience. We

---

73 Hopko, *Winter Pascha*, 93.

recognize that it is not yet fully manifested in this world but will be so at the return of Christ. It is in the Church that we have the fullness of the foretaste of the Kingdom of God.

Thus Jesus said, "I will build my Church" (Matt. 16:18). His Kingdom is Life, and it is what our life on earth is all about. Belief in Jesus Christ brings us into the Kingdom of God through baptism and makes us its citizens. At the same time, we are made members of His Body, the Church, to be a holy nation unto Him.

Our Ascent to Heaven

Both of these truths, that of worship as heaven on earth and of the Church as the presence of the Kingdom of God, are crucial to understanding the Divine Liturgy in its fullness. As Orthodox Christians, we recognize that worship is an entrance into the dimension of the Kingdom. Further, the Eucharist, which is the focus of the Liturgy, is a sacramental thing—a thing of grace, a thing of the Kingdom that involves "the idea of transformation, which refers to the ultimate event of Christ's death and resurrection, and is always a sacrament of the Kingdom."[74] For the Christian, the Eucharist is not a mere remembrance, a symbolic acting out of an historical event in the life of Jesus Christ. We take our Lord and Savior at His word when He said, "Unless you eat the flesh of the Son of man and drink His blood, you have no life in you. Whoever eats My flesh and drinks My blood has eternal life" (John 6:53–54). In Communion we receive bread and wine that have become the Body and Blood of Christ by the work of the Holy Spirit, by the grace of God. This is what the Scriptures teach.

What actual benefit would there be to a modern memorial service? It does us little or no good; it may stir up feelings of piety, sorrow, or nostalgia, or at best feelings of confident expectation. In contrast, Orthodox Christianity has affirmed from the

---

74 Schmemann, *For the Life of the World,* 81.

beginning that this is real spiritual food, that by partaking of the Body and Blood we are spiritually nurtured. This is indeed a mystery, and it is a thing of grace. Christ is the source of our spiritual life, and it is by the continual partaking of His Body and Blood that we are strengthened and grow spiritually.

The Eucharist is not of this world: it is of the Kingdom. It is the Body and Blood of Him who rules in the Kingdom of God. How can we expect to receive the things of the Kingdom on this earth? For them, we must go to the Kingdom. That is the ultimate purpose of the Divine Liturgy. It is an ascent to heaven, to the Kingdom of God. It is the liturgical and sacramental dynamic of worship that carries us from this world into the dimension of the Kingdom, where we may partake of spiritual things and participate in spiritual worship before the Throne of God.

At a common-sense level, this is simply applying to the Eucharist what Christ expected us to apply to our lives, for as St. Paul enjoins us, "our citizenship is in heaven" (Phil. 3:20). We are to live in a manner that shows our citizenship is in heaven. Applied to our worship, this is likely what Jesus meant when He told the Samaritan woman that "the hour is coming when you will neither on this mountain, nor in Jerusalem, worship the Father," but as He went on to point out to her, "the hour is coming, and now is, when the true worshipers will worship the Father in spirit and truth; for the Father is seeking such to worship Him. God *is* Spirit, and those who worship Him must worship in spirit and truth" (John 4:21–24). The point is quite elementary: worshiping God is not a thing of this world; it is a thing of the Spirit. And if the Kingdom is the place of God, then the Kingdom is where we had better be worshiping "in spirit and truth."

The destination of the Liturgy is known from the outset—the first words said by the priest are "Blessed is the Kingdom of the Father and of the Son and of the Holy Spirit, now and ever, and unto ages of ages." Our destination is the Kingdom of God, where we worship Him in spirit and in truth and join the saints and the host of heaven in worship. Father Schmemann writes:

> To bless the Kingdom is not simply to acclaim it. It is to declare it to be the goal, the end of all our desires and interests, of our whole life, the supreme and ultimate value of all that exists. To bless is to accept in love, and to move toward what is loved and accepted. The Church is thus the assembly, the gathering of those to whom the ultimate destination of all life has been revealed and who have accepted it. This acceptance is expressed in the solemn answer to the doxology: Amen. It is indeed one of the most important words in the world, for it expresses the agreement of the Church to follow Christ in His ascension to His Father, to make this ascension the destiny of man.[75]

Experientially, the Liturgy is an act of divine beauty. To witness and to participate in it and to become aware of its aesthetic value is to become aware of God's love for us. The point of any writing or analysis of the Liturgy is to encourage the reader to experience and appreciate it for its true worth. Its value, of course, is in the lasting spiritual sustenance it provides.

Here is the element that sets the Divine Liturgy apart from all other Christian worship: it is not this-worldly; rather, it is an otherworldly experience. We ascend to heaven, of which we are now citizens and to which we are ultimately destined, to commune with the God who loves us and has shown forth His love for us. There we worship this God and receive His gifts. This is truly what worship was meant to be: the ascent to heaven in the company of the saints to worship and to know God. Thus the hymn immediately after the Eucharist: *We have seen the true light, we have received the Heavenly Spirit, we have found the true faith, worshiping the undivided Trinity, who has saved us.*

---

75 Schmemann, *For the Life of the World*, 28.

Orthodox Christianity has frequently been accused of going to the opposite extreme, of transposing worship into the Kingdom to such a degree that it is in fact no longer worldly. It must be admitted that this is possible and has occurred. Balance is required, and where must we go for this balance? To the Incarnation. Jesus Himself told us that we are in the world but must not be of the world: our citizenship is in heaven (Phil. 3:20). We certainly must strike a balance if we are to do justice to the Incarnation, but denying the heavenly and settling for the earthly is not balance.

In his treatise on the history and development of the Liturgy, Gregory Dix contended that the effects of scholasticism and centralized authoritarianism in the Church of the West resulted in a crisis regarding the nature of the Eucharist. There came the loss of the eschatological dimension, the Kingdom dimension, from the Eucharist.[76] The Liturgy, and worship in general, was "brought down" from the Kingdom of God to the world.

These understandings continued in the West in Roman Catholicism and became part of the controversy of the Reformation. The net result is that both Roman Catholicism and Protestantism share a more rational, earthly perspective and understanding of worship. This distance from the Kingdom of God and the sacraments never came into Orthodoxy. Orthodox Christianity never left its Kingdom-centeredness, never brought worship and the Eucharist down to earth for examination on our terms. This is not to say that Orthodoxy never developed its own problems that required correction. But, in this crucial area of attention to the Kingdom of God, the Church did not waver.

The Kingdom is not a faraway and abstract concept for the Orthodox Christian. It is the spiritual reality that is life. It is the goal not only of the Divine Liturgy: it is the ultimate goal to which we strive as the children of God. It is our destination.

---

76 Dix, *Shape of the Liturgy*, 621ff.

PART II

✠

A Journey
through the Liturgy

CHAPTER 6

The Interior of an Orthodox Church

WE COME NOW TO A consideration of the celebration of the Divine Liturgy itself, a journey through the full order of this great sacramental action performed by priest and people in co-celebration. Before we set out upon this journey, however, it is important to spend a few moments looking carefully at the place where our actual ascent to the Kingdom is to begin—at the arrangement of the interior of the sanctuary itself.

To those unfamiliar with the internal arrangements of an Orthodox Church building, a first encounter can be surprising and confusing—and exciting. Passing through the door from the outside into the narthex, one is struck by several sights and scents that may be unfamiliar—stands bearing flickering candles and icons depicting the Mother of God and her Divine Child, the saint to whom the church is dedicated, and others. This can be seen in the photo of the interior of an Orthodox church on the following page. There are ornate lamps hanging before the icons, casting their flickering light mysteriously upon the saintly faces. The air is fragrant with the sweet scent of incense drifting in from the interior of the main church. As one passes through the next door into the nave or body of the church proper, the senses are further delighted by color, sound, and scent.

Stained glass and painted icons depict the Lord, His Blessed

Mother, and the saints and portray events from His earthly life. One may also hear the sound of chanting from choir or cantor. These things are not decorations, nor are they irrelevant embellishments piled one upon the other like the clutter of centuries. They are instead deeply significant sacramental aids to worship and are used deliberately to create the *ambience sacrée*—the holy atmosphere that addresses the entire human being—directing all of the human senses toward the sweetness of God. For a human being is incomplete if viewed only as an immortal soul. The body, as well as the spirit, is needed to constitute the complete being. And the body has senses whereby the whole being becomes aware of its surroundings. These senses are soothed, sanctified with holy sights, sounds, and scents so that they, too, may delight in the Lord. "Oh, taste and see that the LORD *is* good" (Ps. 33/34:8).

The church building is frequently—though not invariably—fashioned in the form of a cross. Where this is the case, the foot of the cross is at the western end, where the people enter. At the eastern end a screen bearing icons stands between the main body of the church (the nave) and the eastern extremity where the altar table is located (the sanctuary). This screen may be tall and run completely across the width of the nave, or it may be waist high; it may appear as a solid wall or look more like a screen with icons suspended on it; it may have double doors in the center or be open in the center and thus partially separate the nave from the sanctuary. Such differences are generally the result of cultural or local traditions.

The screen is called the *iconostasis* (icon stand) and bears an array of holy images that are arranged in a fairly consistent order. Three doors penetrate the typical iconostasis: small doors at the north and south ends and a larger, usually double door in the center. In churches with an iconostasis with an open center area there are still generally two small doors on either side. These are called respectively the north door, the south door, and the royal doors. During services, they are open in order that events taking place at the altar may be seen clearly by the congregation. At other times they are closed, protecting the inner sanctuary—the place of the Kingdom—from disturbance.

Certain of the icons on the icon stand occupy the same positions in every parish. As one faces the stand, looking east toward the altar, an icon of the Lord Jesus Christ stands to the right of the royal doors. To the right again stands the icon of St. John the Baptist—the Holy Forerunner—who prepared the way of the Lord. On the south door is an icon of Archangel Michael, and to the right again is at least one other icon of a saint. To the left of the royal doors is an icon of Mary, the Mother of God, with her Divine Child, and to the left again the saint to whom the church is dedicated. On the north door is an icon of the Archangel Gabriel, and one or more variable icons are found to its left. Above the royal doors is generally an icon of the Last Supper—depicting the institution of the Sacrament of Holy Communion. The various doors in the icon stand give access to and from the sanctuary or altar area. The royal doors are reserved for the passage of the bishop, priests, and deacons. Other assistants such as subdeacons and acolytes pass through the north and south doors.

As one looks through the royal doors into the holy sanctuary, the altar table on which the Holy Eucharist is celebrated stands centrally. To the side is a small table covered by a white cloth, upon which the Holy Gifts—the bread and wine to be used in the Eucharist—will be prepared by the priest and deacon. This preparation table is called the *prothesis*. Behind the altar in most Orthodox churches stands the bishop's throne, occupied by the bishop during his pastoral visitations to the parish. In Greek and Antiochian Orthodox churches, however, this throne is frequently located in front of the icon screen to the right of the royal doors, in the wide area before the screen known as the *solea*.

The presence of a bishop's throne in a parish church, rather than only in a cathedral as in the West, emphasizes the central role of the bishop as the ruling figure of Christ in his diocese and the subordinate role of the presbyter or priest as his delegated deputy. The continuing core of apostolicity resides in the bishop, who was ordained via the laying on of hands by a bishop, who in turn was ordained by a bishop whose ordination goes back in an unbroken line to the apostles. Where the bishop is enthroned, surrounded by his presbyters, deacons, and people—there is the fullness, the catholicity of the Church. The presence of the throne makes this visually clear.

At the eastern end of the church, above the altar, there is in many Orthodox traditions (but not invariably) a great icon of the Mother of God, always with her Divine Son. In this icon the Virgin Mary generally has her arms outstretched as if to embrace the whole of creation as a loving mother. In this act she gathers all things to her beloved Son and offers Him to the whole world. This icon is often called the *Platytéra Tôn Ouranôn*, or "she who embraces all the heavens." A majestic sight indeed—the Incarnate

Word and His Mother, God and humanity, radiating love and benediction and drawing all eyes to the altar, to the place where the divine Kingdom will be actualized.

In the solea, the open space before the icon stand, the Sacraments of the Church are administered to the people. Here the Holy Eucharist is received; here the death and rebirth of Holy Baptism occurs at the baptismal font; here, kneeling before the icon of Christ in judgment, the penitent kneels and redirects his steps toward God; here too the sacrament of matrimony is performed and couples are married—the two becoming one flesh in Christ. In this general area before the icon screen there may be located chanter stands (sometimes one, occasionally one on either side), and often to one side a speaker's stand or pulpit from which homilies or sermons are delivered. On occasion there may be a simple lectern or stand from which the Scriptures are read. Again, such variations reflect custom or cultural tradition rather than any doctrinal position.

As we saw in Part I, the Jewish synagogue had a bema or raised platform, and this came into early Eastern and Western churches as a raised platform from which the Scriptures were read. It was called the *ambon*, from the Greek word meaning "elevated place." These structures varied in degrees of elaborateness from simple wooden platforms to enormous and highly decorated affairs such as that in the Church of Hagia Sophia in Constantinople, which was large enough to accommodate a number of people and upon which some of the Byzantine Emperors were crowned. While the ambon persists in many traditional Orthodox churches, in Russian and other Slavic churches it tends to be represented by a small extension in front of the icon screen on which is placed a lectern from which the Scriptures are read.

Where the church is designed in the form of a cross, the north and south arms constitute two transepts generally adorned with icons or windows. In Greek churches the *epitaphion* may be kept here. This is a movable bier, a depiction of the sepulchre of Christ where an icon of Christ is laid on good Friday, when the tomb is frequently decorated with flowers, according to local custom. It is used in processions during the services of Holy Week.

Sights, sounds, scents—all the senses are addressed, and the whole being is exalted. "O Lord, I love the beauty of Your house, / And the place where Your glory dwells" (Ps. 25:8 OSB). Every wall, every window, every arch and column show forth the glory of God and His Kingdom. The interior of the church is, however, but the gateway to the Kingdom. It is the point of departure where the gathered faithful—the people of God, the mystical Body of Christ together with their priest—begin their ascent to the royal table where the Eucharist is actualized and this world is for a time left totally behind. And it is for this reason, therefore, that there are all of these things that create the ambience of holiness. For here truly is the gate of heaven, the very passage that leads us before the Throne.

CHAPTER 7

The Preparation Service

THE DIVINE LITURGY MAY BE seen as falling naturally into three parts—the Rite of Preparation, the Liturgy of the Word, and the Eucharist. During the Rite of Preparation, preliminary prayers are recited before the icon stand, the priests and deacons put on their vestments, and the bread and wine which are to be actualized as the Body and Blood of Christ are made ready for their transformation.

The Liturgy of the Word consists of petitionary prayers and supplications, psalms, and the reading of the Epistle and Gospel, followed by a sermon or homily. The final portion is the Eucharist, in which the ascent to the Kingdom is consummated, the bread and wine are consecrated, and the assembly receives the Holy Communion. We will begin with the Rite of Preparation.

On entering the church prior to the preparation of the bread and wine, priests and deacons stand before the icon screen and recite what are called the Trisagion prayers. These include a prayer to the Holy Spirit, a prayer to the Holy Trinity, and the Lord's Prayer. After this, priest and deacon bow to the people and enter the sanctuary—the priest through the south door and the deacon through the north door. As they enter, both recite Psalm 5:

I will enter into Your house; I will bow down in Your Holy Temple in Your fear.

Hide me, Lord, with Your righteousness; because of my enemies, make straight my path before You.

For there is no truth in their mouths; their hearts are vain: their thoughts are as an open grave; they have dealt deceitfully with their tongues.

Judge them, O God, let them fall from their devices.

According to the multitude of their iniquities, cast them out, for they have provoked You exceedingly.

And let all be joyful who trust in You; they shall rejoice forever, and You shall dwell in them; and those who love Your name shall glory in You.

For You, O Lord, will bless a just man; with the shield of benevolence have you crowned us.

The priest and deacon now approach the altar, bow before it, and kiss the altar and the hand cross. They have entered the holy sanctuary only after prayers of purification at the gate of the Kingdom. Supplicatory prayers are said to invoke the Holy Spirit, that He might dwell within them and within the people. Other prayers are directed to all three Persons of the Holy Trinity in the ancient prayer of the thrice-holy hymn—the Trisagion—in which the three Persons are addressed, "Holy God, Holy Mighty, Holy Immortal One." This is followed by a plea for abiding love, compassion, and understanding: "Have mercy on us."

The recitation of the Lord's Prayer—the prayer of prayers—follows and emphasizes the new and unique relationship that Jesus Christ, by His mediation, has brought about between God and humanity. We are permitted to call the transcendent God "Father." This emphasizes the fact of the new familial relationship between God and mankind, that of father and children, which has been made possible by the death of Jesus Christ. The kissing of the altar and the hand cross emphasize the sanctity of the place where the Lord's Supper is to be celebrated. Reverence for Christ and for His Kingdom are shown forth by this intimate and humble gesture, and similar acts of reverence will be seen throughout the Divine Liturgy by both clergy and people.

The Vesting

Priest and deacon now put on their vestments. The wearing of special vestments for the celebration of temple worship goes far back into Old Testament times. As we have seen, the practice of wearing vestments has its origins in the temple traditions, although in the very early Christian Church the clergy did not wear any distinguishing vestments. Beginning with the retention of civilized clothing, and with the rapid liturgical developments of the third through the fifth centuries, vestments were adopted to signify the role of the clergy (specifically of the priest as icon of Christ) and to show forth the beauty of the Kingdom. The nature and appearance of these vestments have undergone significant change over time, but these changes have become hallowed by long usage; each article of vestiture has acquired its own meaning and purpose that is sacramental rather than ceremonial.

First, the priest puts on a long garment with sleeves, called the *sticharion* (tunic). This vestment, which reaches to the floor, evolved from the ancient tunic that was the universal garment of the classical world, common to all classes of society. In the context of the Church, the wearing of the tunic by the priest has come to signify purity of conscience and of the life conferred by the Holy Spirit. The deacon also wears a tunic, but its sleeves are wide, whereas those of the priest are close fitting. After donning the tunic, the priest puts on the stole (*epitrachelion*). This word means "upon the neck" and describes how the vestment is worn—as a loop around the neck. The two halves of this broad, strap-like vestment are sewn together in front and hang down to the floor. This permanent union of the two halves of the vestment may indicate the two natures of Christ—human and divine—and the two offices of priest and deacon.

Wearing the garment about the neck indicates putting on the yoke of Christ, the willingness to bear suffering and sacrifice for His sake and for the sake of the flock. The lower ends of the garment often terminate in a fringe, the individual filaments of which may represent the people for whom the priest is spiritually responsible. The stole worn by the deacon (*orarion*), is simpler and narrower than that of the priest, being a long narrow band that is worn hanging down over the left shoulder. The stole is required to be worn for the performance of any liturgical office. Its origin is somewhat obscure but is known to have originated early in the life of the Church. In contrast to the other vestments, which derived from common dress, the stole was probably used when clergy still wore everyday clothing: the stole was then the only sign of the clerical office.

The priest's long, loose-fitting tunic is secured at the waist by a girdle (*zoné*). This is a belt-like vestment made of brocaded material and tied at the back. Practically, it gathers together the tunic at the waist and controls it. Liturgically, putting on the girdle indicates readiness and preparedness for spiritual combat and spiritual trial (John 13:4, Eph. 6:14). The sleeves of the tunic are now gathered at the wrist by special cuffs (*epimanikia*). This word simply means "about the wrists" and signifies their function. These almost certainly evolved from ancient Byzantine imperial dress and were later adopted by bishops and ultimately by priests also. Liturgically, they have come to indicate the strength and the power of God, made manifest through the office of His priest.

In classical times, a garment was worn over the tunic as a heavier outer covering. It was long at the back and sides like a cloak, while descending in front down to the waist. It had no sleeves and a single opening for the head. Poor people generally made this garment out of coarse, thick material and wore it primarily for protection against inclement weather or for traveling in cold seasons. Those better off had it made of richer stuffs—silks and brocades, for example—so that it became for them less functional as an all-weather garment and more of an ornament attesting to their economic status.

This cloak-like garment, the chasuble (*phelonion*), has been preserved as one of the most important of the priestly vestments. Like its ancient counterpart, it is worn over the tunic, but its protective function, in liturgical terms, is very different from merely shielding the wearer from the weather. Putting on this garment, which is the final act in the process of vesting, indicates spiritual readiness. Specific prayers have been said as each garment is put on, and additional preparatory prayers will be said before the start of the Liturgy. Why is this necessary? Simply because prayer is requisite for worship.

Bishops wear a vestment over the chasuble that consists of a long strip of similar material adorned with crosses and arranged about the bishop's shoulders in such a manner that one end descends in front and the other behind. This vestment is called the *omophorion*—literally, "borne on the shoulders"—and probably evolved from the ancient *omophorion* worn especially by old people as an additional protective covering. Originally, it was a sheepskin or fleece; this was later replaced by a long dyed woolen garment, which in turn evolved into the garment worn today, which is fashioned of the same materials as the other principal vestments. The omophorion serves to remind the bishop of his duty to promote the Faith, to bring about the propagation of the Faith as a merciful shepherd would seek after and bring back his lost sheep. Clearly, the origin of this garment and its evolution from a simple sheepskin focus attention on the role of the bishop as shepherd of the flock.

Before the Divine Liturgy, as each vestment is put on, the

priest prays and blesses it, so that all components of his vestiture become not adornments, nor a uniform, nor the regalia of office, but truly sacramental implements necessary to the proper performance of his priestly office. After vesting, he stands now within the sanctuary, clothed in the grace of the Holy Spirit, which we perceive in the tunic; girded for combat in the constant, invisible warfare against the powers of darkness, as shown by the girdle; his wrists and hands strengthened by the very priestly power of Christ Himself, made manifest in the cuffs; shielded and guarded from the baneful influences of the adversary by the mighty shield of God Himself, as manifested by the chasuble. He stands reverently, with humility, but also with the invincible strength of Jesus Christ. He is the icon of Christ, and for the Liturgy about to be celebrated he becomes for us Christ Himself.

The Preparation of the Bread and Wine

The priest (and deacon, if one is present) proceed now to the preparation table. This is located generally at the north end of the sanctuary. They make three small bows before the table and say:

God, be merciful to me a sinner (Luke 18:13).

You have redeemed us from the curse of the law (Gal. 3:13) by Your precious blood. Nailed to the cross and pierced with a lance, You have bestowed immortality upon mankind. Our Savior, glory be to You.

On the table of preparation are the Gifts, the offerings of bread and wine, which are to be consecrated during the great eucharistic rite of the Divine Liturgy. Frequently, if one searches among the decorations of an Orthodox Church, one may find pictures depicting ears of wheat and bunches of grapes. From these humble fruits of the earth are fashioned bread and wine, principal staples of daily food. Bread and wine—how simple, how commonplace these things appear. Yet it is just these mundane elements of our daily food, from which our very bodies replenish themselves, that will be offered back to God in the mystery of the Divine Liturgy and that will in turn be returned to us transformed into the very Body and Blood of the Savior.

For it is these very simple elements that, when consumed by humans, are turned into the very flesh and blood of those who consume them. And it is these same simple elements that, at the holy consecration in the most sacred moment of the Liturgy—the *epiklesis,* or invocation of the Holy Spirit—will themselves be transformed for us into the very Body and Blood of Jesus Christ. Consider two ears of wheat, two clusters of grapes. Both are plucked and then turned into bread and wine. One, perhaps, will be the simple food of humble people, but the other may be exalted beyond infinity—to become the very Body and Blood of the Savior. "Thine own of Thine own we offer to Thee, on behalf of all and for all things." These words the priest will speak as the consecration approaches, when the bloodless sacrifice of the Eucharist is about to be accomplished. Bread and wine—so simple, so ordinary—destined to become immeasurable treasures of inestimable worth. And all this is to begin with the Rite of Preparation.

In the early Church, before Christianity became widespread, the Rite of Preparation was an act of the people. Prior to the Liturgy, the people would bring their gifts, their sacrifices, to offer to God. These would be all manner of things, including bread and wine. The primary function of the deacon was the distribution of these gifts to the needy in the church (see Acts 7). From among those gifts brought, the deacons selected and brought the bread and wine, the gifts to be offered in the Eucharist. Thus we see that the understanding of sacrifice and thanksgiving were intimately tied together in the thought and action of the people. Their gifts to God were in fact the gifts offered; their sacrifices offered became part of Christ's sacrifice. And this action on the part of the community actualized the prayer "Thine own of Thine own we offer Thee."

This explains in part why non-Orthodox Christians are asked not to partake of the Eucharist. Orthodox Christians believe that the Eucharist is a sacramental grace, whereby the bread and wine become the Body and Blood of Jesus Christ, by which we are spiritually nurtured. This is an understanding not shared by many Christians, to their loss. However, since it is the Body and Blood of Jesus Christ, it should be received only by those who believe and anticipate it as such. And as we saw in Part I, the Orthodox Church sees no distinction between the Body of the risen Christ and His eucharistic Body, the Church. Thus when we receive the Eucharist, we receive the Church: that is, the Head and all its members, the Lord, the Virgin Mary, all the saints who are in the Church. This understanding of the Eucharist demands a very different approach to Holy Communion. Such no doubt was the intent in St. Paul's mind when he wrote:

> Therefore whoever eats this bread or drinks *this* cup of the Lord in an unworthy manner will be guilty of the body and blood of the Lord. But let a man examine himself, and so let him eat of the bread and drink of the cup. For he who eats and drinks in an unworthy manner eats and drinks judgment to himself, not discerning the Lord's body. (1 Cor. 11:27–29)

The other part of the reason is historical. When the Roman Catholic Church split from the Orthodox Church in the eleventh century, the result was a break in communion. Because a fundamental change in the understanding of God was involved, communion was broken. Members of the Roman Church could not receive communion in an Orthodox Church and vice versa. And Protestant Christians, as the offspring of Rome, are *de facto* outside of the communion of the Orthodox Church.

Perhaps one day this splintering in Christendom will be healed.

The bread used in the Holy Eucharist is made simply from flour and water, and it is leavened. Only fresh loaves are used. These loaves are called *prosphora*, a Greek word simply meaning "offerings." On the top of each loaf is the symbol of a cross with the Greek letters IC XC NI KA inscribed into the four corners of the cross. This is imprinted by means of a wooden bread stamp, which is pressed into the dough and removed after the loaves have risen.

This inscription is an abbreviation for "Jesus Christ conquers" and summarizes the vision seen by the Emperor Constantine on the eve of his great victory over the pagan Maxentius at the Milvian Bridge. In this vision Constantine understood that under the sign of Christ he would conquer. Traditionally, five loaves were used in a Divine Liturgy, recalling the five loaves that Christ took and multiplied to feed the multitude (Matt. 14:13). The wine used is generally a sweet red wine, and it must be in perfect condition.

In the very early days of the Church the Holy Eucharist was still celebrated in the context of a ritual meal, deriving as we have seen from the Passover meal of the Jews. As the understanding of the new Passover, or *Pascha*, grew, the ritual meal became widely known as *agape*, a feast of love. The bread and wine, which would be consecrated and so become the Body and Blood of Jesus Christ in the Eucharist, were brought as offerings by members of the faithful in addition to the other items of food originally provided for the meal. Here again, as the Church grew in numbers, logistics became a problem. It became difficult to provide the Eucharist in the context of a meal, and this was heightened by problems such as those in the church at Corinth.

The ritual meal was reduced to a small fragment of the prosphora, blessed but not consecrated. This practice is still followed today: a piece of blessed but unconsecrated bread is distributed to each person after they receive Communion and again when they leave the church at the end of the Liturgy. This bread was originally known as the *evlogia*, the blessed bread—not to be confused with the eucharistic gifts of the altar. In late Byzantine usage, it became known as *antidoron*—a word meaning "instead of the gifts," perhaps carrying with it the implication that if one did not receive Communion then this was perhaps better than nothing. It is worthwhile to mention both terms, since both may be encountered in Orthodox churches of various traditions. But it must be emphasized that in no way can a simple piece of bread be regarded as any kind of alternative to receiving Holy Communion. Rather, we would prefer to think of it as the remains of the *agape*, the common meal of the early Church. For this reason, we would strongly recommend avoiding the term *antidoron* in favor of the earlier term *evlogia*.

The opening prayer of the Rite of Preparation, "God be merciful to me, a sinner," is an appeal to God for blessing and compassion. It is in this spirit of humility and penitence that the Liturgy begins with the preparation of the gifts. With a series of prayers and petitions, the priest and deacon now bless the bread and cut it into pieces. The prayers and petitions recall the sacrifice on Calvary—the reconciling act of Jesus Christ. The bread is cut in a ritualistic manner, and the pieces commemorate the Lamb of God, Mary the Mother of God, the angelic host, the martyrs, the confessors, the ascetics, the healers, and all the saints—living and dead—as well as the celebrant himself. Thus the entire Church is represented in the bread, and it is the entire Body that we receive in the Eucharist.

The wine, which is mixed with water in the chalice, recalls the outpouring of water and blood from Christ's side on the Cross, symbolic of the outpouring of grace upon humanity and the reconciliation to God which it makes possible. This Rite of Preparation has commemorated all aspects of the Church, its origin, its continued history, and its ultimate and eternal dimension of the heavenly Kingdom. The pieces of bread, which have been cut out of the loaf, are placed on the paten (*diskos*) and covered with a little star-like cover (*asteriskos*). In so doing, the star, which paused above the stable at Bethlehem, showing forth the place of the Savior's birth, is commemorated. The paten and chalice are then covered with the veil (*aer*), acknowledging the investment of Christ in divine glory. The veil is used to cover the sacred gifts and to perform other functions that will be touched upon as we progress through the fascinating course of the Liturgy.

Finally, the Rite of Preparation is concluded with the censing of the sacred Gifts. Taking the censer with burning incense, the priest censes the covered Gifts, praying that the Lord will bless these offerings and accept them on behalf of those who offer them and of those for whom they are offered. All is now ready to move into the second phase of the Divine Liturgy—the Liturgy of the Word.

CHAPTER 8

The Liturgy of the Word

THE DIVINE LITURGY MOVES FORWARD into the Liturgy of the Word, which is made up of psalmody, readings from the Scriptures (Epistle and Gospel), and a sermon or homily for the instruction of the faithful, usually based on the Gospel text of the day. As we have seen, these elements of worship came directly from synagogue worship.

Depending upon tradition or local custom, the office of Matins (*Orthros*) may be celebrated prior to the Divine Liturgy. If so, the Rite of Preparation may be concluded before Matins begins. (If sufficient clergy are present, they may take place concurrently.) Connecting this part of the Liturgy with the Rite of Preparation that has just ended is a short intervening opening phase, which was certainly recognizable as early as the eighth century but is probably much older. This part of the Liturgy is known technically as the *enarxis*, and simply served as a smooth connection between the preparatory and instructional parts. Although it is now generally included in the Liturgy of the Word, it should be realized that in the earlier Church it was not well-defined, and the Liturgy of the Word actually began with a procession in which the deacon, the presbyters (priests, elders), and the bishop entered the sanctuary bearing the Gospel book. Today this survives and is called the Little Entrance. The office of Matins concludes with the Great Doxology. If Matins is not celebrated directly before the Divine Liturgy, then this is sung at the outset of the Liturgy. This is an all-embracing hymn of praise and thanksgiving to the Holy Trinity. It is very ancient in origin and is a fitting starting point for all Christian worship.

Following the Great Doxology, the priest stands at the altar and lifts the Gospel book in his hands. The deacon stands in the solea directly before the Royal Doors, where he will soon begin to chant a series of petitions to God. The people will respond to the deacon's verbalization of the Church's petitions with the words "Lord, have mercy" (*Kyrie eleison*). The words that actually begin the Divine Liturgy are not heard by the congregation, as they are prayers that the priest and deacon offer at the altar. These are said during the chanting of the Great Doxology. Having concluded their prayers, the priest kisses the altar and the Gospel.

> DEACON: *It is time for the Lord to act. Father, give the blessing.*
>
> The priest, raising the Gospel book and making the sign of the cross with it over the altar, chants in a loud voice:
>
> PRIEST: *Blessed is the Kingdom of the Father and of the Son and of the Holy Spirit, now and ever and unto ages of ages.*
>
> DEACON AND PEOPLE: *Amen.*

This is the opening sign of the cross, through which our awareness of the saving nature of Christ's sacrifice is expressed and realized. As the priest blesses the altar with the Gospel book, so the people bless themselves by making the sign of the Cross. In the Eastern Orthodox tradition, this is done with the right hand, with the thumb, index, and middle fingers joined together at the tips. These three digits represent the three Divine Persons of the Trinity. Also, the ring and little fingers are folded across the palm, signifying the two natures—divine and human—of Jesus Christ.

In making the sign, the three conjoined digits are touched first to the forehead, secondly to the breast, thirdly to the right shoulder, and finally to the left shoulder. Unlike the Western practice, the sign of the Cross is made from right to left. This may signify that the truth of God passed from the Children of Israel (on the right hand of God) to the Gentiles (on the left hand of God). This appears to have been a universal practice in both East and West prior to the reign of Pope Innocent III at the beginning of the thirteenth century, when most of the blessing was changed in the West from left to right, and made with the whole hand with all fingers joined together. It should be recognized that making the sign of the Cross is not merely a ritualistic maneuver. To bless is to acknowledge and proclaim; to make the sign of the Cross is to acknowledge the reality of the Kingdom before us. As the Incarnation signifies, the coming of Christ was to redeem body and spirit, an integrated redemption. Making the sign of the Cross involves the body and the spirit in a direct act of prayer.

The priest's actions are incredibly significant, for he *blesses the Kingdom*. This blessing of the Heavenly Kingdom serves to declare it, to show it forth; to envision it not as remote paradise or utopian dream world but as very Kingdom of God proclaimed and actualized by Jesus Himself. To bless the Kingdom is to proclaim it to be the aim and purpose of all existence: the *raison d'etre* of our lives. And this opening blessing proclaims that it is to this Kingdom that we shall ascend for a while during the Divine Liturgy—not symbolically but *actually*. During this sacred time, we shall ascend to the Throne, and it is to the assembled people of God, gathered together in the name of Christ to actualize and make whole the Church, that this declaration is made. The people of God acknowledge it and express their acceptance of it by signing themselves with the Cross and pronouncing the word *amen*, "let it be so," with a loud and joyful shout.

This coming together of the people of God is above all a joyous one. There is a sense of excitement, an anticipation of the glorious things to come. For the people are gathered together to enter for a time into the dimension of the Kingdom, to journey to the next world. They will leave behind for a short time the cares and pre-occupations of this world and will stand before the very heavenly Table and will partake of the heavenly banquet. The gathering of the people around their deacons and priests and their bishop is the actualization of the Church and proclaims it to be catho-lic, for in the Eastern Orthodox tradition the word *catholic* does not have merely the meaning of geographic universality. On the contrary, it derives from the Greek words *kath olon*, which mean "concerning the whole" or "concerning completeness." That is to say, that which is catholic is complete and entire, lacking noth-ing. And, as St. Ignatius of Antioch (d. AD 107) proclaimed in his *Epistle to the Magnesians*, wherever such a gathering comes together, there is the fullness of the Catholic Church.[77] Thus it is here as with every part of the Divine Liturgy: a seeming outward simplicity expresses the deepest, profoundest, and most glorious of truths.

The Great Litany

There now follows the Great Litany, a series of petitions chanted by the deacon and responded to by the people in which all catego-ries of human need are addressed. The deacon leaves the sanctu-ary through the north door, and standing before the Royal Doors chants each petition loudly, lifting his stole as each one is sung and bowing slightly towards the altar. To each of these petitions, as we have said above, the people respond, "Lord, have mercy."

---

77 St. Ignatius of Antioch, "Epistle to the Magnesians," in *Patrologia Graeca*, ed. Jacques-Paul Migne (Paris: Imprimerie Catholique, 1857–66), 3:71d.

The litany begins thus:

DEACON: *In peace let us pray to the Lord.*

PEOPLE: *Lord, have mercy.*

DEACON: *For the peace from above and for the salvation of our souls, let us pray to the Lord.*

This antiphonal prayer continues between the deacon and the people, with the people responding "Lord, have mercy" to each petition.

DEACON: *For the peace of the whole world, for the stability of the holy churches of God, and for the union of all, let us pray to the Lord.*

For this holy house and for all who enter with faith, reverence, and the fear of God, let us pray to the Lord.

For our Metropolitan (name), for the honorable priests and deacons in Christ, and for all the clergy and the people, let us pray to the Lord

For this country and for every authority and power within it, let us pray to the Lord

For this city, for every city and country and for the faithful living in them, let us pray to the Lord.

For seasonable weather, for an abundance of the fruits of the earth, and for peaceful times, let us pray to the Lord.

For those who travel by land, air, and sea, the sick and suffering, those under persecution and for their deliverance, let us pray to the Lord.

For our deliverance from affliction, anger, danger, and need, let us pray to the Lord.

Help us, save us, have mercy on us and keep us, O God, by
Your grace.

The litany concludes with this petition:

DEACON: *Remembering our most holy, most pure, most*
blessed and glorious Lady, the Mother of God, and
Ever-Virgin Mary, with all the saints, let us commit our-
selves and each other and all our life unto Christ our God.

PEOPLE: *To you, O Lord.*

The initial petitionary prayers of the faithful are for the two things
we desire most: the peace of God and our salvation. Why these?
Because the peace of God is what we need and desire most as we
strive to live out our lives on this earth. Indeed, it is only in the
peace of Jesus Christ that we may live a Christian life, let alone
approach the Throne of God. We likewise pray for salvation, for
it was what Christ came to make available to us and is the goal to
which we strive. We pray for our salvation regularly, for it is a process: we have been saved, we are being saved, and we will be saved
in Jesus Christ. These two opening petitions set the tone not only
of this litany but also of the Divine Liturgy as a whole.

This litany is known technically as the *Great Ektenia*, which
is to say, something rather long and extended. The litany covers
every aspect of human need. It prays for the Church, the world,
for the whole of creation. It pleads for our release from the trials
and tribulations of our daily lives. It is not only the deacon but
all the people who offer these petitions and after each one request
God's mercy.

The word *mercy* in English is the translation of the Greek word
eleos, and it has the same ultimate root as the old Greek word for
oil, or more precisely, olive oil, a substance that was used exten-
sively as a soothing agent for bruises and minor wounds. The oil
was poured onto the wound and gently massaged in, thus soothing, comforting, and making whole the injured part (see the

parable of the Good Samaritan, Luke 10:33). The Hebrew word that is translated as *eleos* (mercy) is *hesed*, which means "steadfast love." The Greek words for "Lord, have mercy," are *Kyrie eleison*—that is to say, "Lord, soothe me, comfort me, take away my pain, show me Your steadfast love and Your compassion."

Thus, the word *mercy* does not refer so much to justice or acquittal—a very Western interpretation—but to the infinite loving-kindness of God and His compassion for His suffering children. It is in this sense that we pray "Lord, have mercy" with great frequency throughout the Divine Liturgy.

The Antiphons

As the deacon is concluding the Great Litany with a commemoration of the Blessed Virgin Mary and the saints, the priest at the altar (or in some traditions priest and people together) recites the prayer of the First Antiphon:

> PRIEST: *O Lord our God, whose power is unimaginable and whose glory is inconceivable, whose mercy is immeasurable and whose love for mankind is beyond all words, in Your compassion, Lord, look down on us and on this holy house, and grant us and those who are praying with us the riches of Your mercy and compassion. For to You are due all glory, honor, and worship, to the Father and to the Son and to the Holy Spirit, now and ever and unto ages of ages.*

DEACON AND PEOPLE: *Amen.*

> The deacon now makes a small bow, moves to stand before the icon of Christ on the icon screen, and raises his stole with his right hand while the choir and people sing the First Antiphon:

Through the prayers of the Mother of God. O Savior, save us.

Sing joyfully to the Lord, all the earth; sing to His name, give glory to His praise.

Through the prayers of the Mother of God, O Savior, save us.

Let all the earth adore Thee and sing unto Thee; let us sing unto Thy name, O Most High!

Glory to the Father and to the Son and to the Holy Spirit, now and ever and unto ages of ages. Amen.

This is the first of the three antiphons, chants that were developed in the very early Church. We saw previously that their origin was in the singing of psalms by the people when they assembled outside the church waiting for the beginning of the Liturgy. The antiphonal responses, wherein the cantor chanted a psalm verse and the people responded with the same refrain, were probably in place by the fourth or fifth century. The cantor would then continue with the second verse, to which the people responded, and so on. This is evident in the First Antiphon, in which the first verses of Psalm 63 are alternated with an appeal to the Theotokos for her intercession. In some traditions the psalm refrains are not sung every Sunday, but only on feast days. These verses are particularly fitting at the beginning of the Divine Liturgy, for they invite all people to praise the Lord for the mightiness of His works.

At the conclusion of the First Antiphon the deacon returns to his former place before the Royal Doors, bows slightly, and begins the Little Litany:

DEACON: *Again and again in peace let us pray to the Lord.*

PEOPLE: *Lord, have mercy.*

DEACON: *Help us, save us, have mercy on us, and keep us, O God, by Thy grace.*

PEOPLE: *Lord, have mercy.*

DEACON: *Remembering our most holy, most pure, most blessed, and glorious Lady, the Mother of God and Ever-Virgin Mary, with all the saints, let us commit ourselves and each other and all our lives unto Christ our God.*

PEOPLE: *To Thee, O Lord.*

In some traditions the Little Litany is shortened to this:

DEACON: *Again and again, let us pray to the Lord.*

PEOPLE: *Lord, have mercy.*

At this juncture the priest (or in some traditions priest and people, as with the First Antiphon) says the prayer of the Second Antiphon:

PRIEST: *O Lord our God, save Your people and bless Your inheritance. Guard the fullness of Your Church, sanctify those who love the beauty of Your house, glorify them by Your Divine power, and do not forsake us who hope in You. For Yours is the dominion and the Kingdom and the power and the glory of the Father and of the Son and of the Holy Spirit, now and ever and unto ages of ages.*

DEACON AND PEOPLE: *Amen.*

The deacon bows slightly, then moves to face the icon of the Theotokos at the left of the Royal Doors. In response to the prayer of the Second Antiphon, the choir and people then sing the Second Antiphon:

O Son of God, who rose from the dead, save us who sing to You, Alleluia.

O God be gracious to us and bless us; make the light of Thy countenance to shine upon us.

O Son of God, who rose from the dead, save us who sing to You, Alleluia.

That we may know Thy way upon the earth, Thy salvation among all nations.

Glory to the Father and to the Son and to the Holy Spirit, now and ever and unto ages of ages. Amen.

Immediately following the conclusion of the Second Antiphon, the choir and people sing the hymn Only-Begotten Son of God:

O only-begotten Son and Word of God, although You are immortal, yet for our salvation You condescended to be made flesh by the holy Mother of God and Ever-Virgin Mary. Without undergoing change You became a man and were crucified, trampling down death by death. O Christ our God, who are One of the Holy Trinity and are glorified with the Father and the Holy Spirit, save us!

This prayer, probably written by the Byzantine Emperor Justinian, dates from the sixth century and provides a striking summary of the redemptive work of Christ.

In preparation for the prayer of the Third Antiphon the deacon now moves in front of the Royal Doors and once again chants the Little Litany. In some traditions this is again shortened to this:

Deacon: *Let us pray to the Lord.*

People: *Lord, have mercy.*

Then the priest—or priest and people, depending upon the tradition—says the prayer of the Third Antiphon.

Priest: *O Lord, who has given us the grace to pray together in peace and harmony, and who promises to grant the requests of two or three who agree in Your name, fulfill even now the petitions of Your servants as is best for us, giving us in this age the knowledge of Your truth, and in the age to come, eternal life.*

The priest concludes the prayer with the Little Doxology:

PRIEST: *For You are good, O our God, and You love mankind, and we send up glory to You, to the Father and to the Son and to the Holy Spirit, now and ever and unto ages of ages.*

DEACON AND PEOPLE: *Amen.*

The composition of the Third Antiphon varies from tradition to tradition. In the Russian church it is regularly the Beatitudes; in others the Troparion of the Resurrection may be substituted. All sing together as follows:

Blessed are the poor in spirit, for theirs is the kingdom of heaven.

Blessed are those who mourn, for they shall be comforted.

Blessed are those who hunger and thirst after righteousness, for they shall be filled.

Blessed are the merciful, for they shall obtain mercy.

Blessed are the pure in heart, for they shall see God.

Blessed are the peacemakers, for they shall be called the children of God.

Blessed are those who are persecuted for righteousness' sake, for theirs is the kingdom of heaven.

Blessed are you when men shall revile you and persecute you and say all manner of evil against you falsely, for My sake.

Rejoice and be glad, for great is your reward in heaven.

With these incomparable words, our Lord began the Sermon on the Mount. In these short sayings, He crystallized clearly for us the manner in which we should live in relation to the world and others. They summarize succinctly the life in Christ. For as He describes these bright faces of blessedness, so He lays before us His own life, His own relationship to the world and to humanity. These are not philosophical precepts born of moralistic musings; on the contrary, they reflect the very life of the Incarnate Word and are a poignant guide for us to emulate, imitate, and live to the fullest extent possible.

In these Beatitudes we are given the conditions for a life of blessedness, of dedication and struggle for Christ's sake, and their fruit is no less than heaven itself. To observe the Beatitudes in our lives is to walk hand-in-hand with Christ Himself, to follow His lead, to bear with Him the Cross, to take the narrow path that always ascends, and to feel the nails in our very flesh, dying to the world and rising again to eternal glory.

Who are the poor in spirit? Those who realize the profound truth that everything they possess, including their very existence, is not really their own but is extended to them in trust from God Himself. Those who are poor in spirit know they have nothing, command nothing, and are capable of nothing without God's continued help and authority. All that we have is on loan from God. All that we achieve is by God's bounty. Those who realize this praise Him in humility and try not to abuse the precious gifts (*charismata*) that have been entrusted to their care.

Those who mourn are not merely those lamenting the departure of a loved one or friend. Those who mourn lament our fallen condition. They weep from their very hearts out of the realization of the great gulf between fallen humanity and the loving God. They have some inkling of the vastness of this chasm, some concept of the dimension of the catastrophe that was the Fall. They weep for their own transgressions and the transgressions of the whole fallen world. They call for compassion, for understanding, for the love of God as a merciful Father. And those who so mourn shall find peace and repose.

And those who are meek as Christ was meek—not promoting themselves with false pride, not vainly raising themselves above their fellows—these shall inherit the riches of the Kingdom. Blessed also are those who hunger and thirst after righteousness—that is, those who devote their lives to the constant quest for God, to love and to serve Him, to fast and to pray, to do good works for His sake, to keep His commandments.

And the pure in heart are those who through their devotion to God invite His presence into their very hearts by surrendering themselves wholly to His love and mercy. By yielding absolutely their whole lives to Him, they possess Him within themselves and are possessed by Him, and thus come to know Him with an indescribable intimacy.

Likewise, blessed are those who suffer persecution for the love of God, patiently enduring pain, suffering, and even death that the Kingdom may be served and brought into being. And blessed are the peacemakers, for peace, forgiveness, and reconciliation actualize the Kingdom.

These three antiphons, with their prayers, short litanies, and praises, were for a long time sung in alternation by two choirs in the larger churches of the Byzantine world. Nowadays, they tend to be shorter and may even be confined to recitation of the prayers of the antiphons themselves. The alternating singing by two choirs, the one answering the other, gave these sung praises their name *antiphon*, literally "opposite" or "alternate" voices. The choirs engaged in a dialogue of praise. The antiphons conclude the beginning rite of the Liturgy of the Word. We now move forward into the service of readings in which the Word of God itself is proclaimed.

The Little Entrance

Priest and deacon now make three small bows before the altar. Then the priest takes the Gospel book from the altar and hands it to the deacon. Then, preceded by candle-bearers, they pass around the back of the altar and exit the sanctuary through the north door. They proceed to the Royal Doors, and the candle-bearers take up positions opposite each other, one before the icon of the Theotokos and the other before the icon of Christ. The priest stands in the middle, with the deacon a little in front and to the right. They bow their heads.

DEACON: *Let us pray to the Lord.*

PRIEST: *O Sovereign Lord, our God, who appointed in heaven the orders and armies of angels and archangels for the service of Your glory, grant that the holy angels may enter with us, to serve and glorify Your goodness with us. For to You are due all glory, honor, and worship, to the Father and to the Son and to the Holy Spirit, now and ever and unto ages of ages.*

The prayer actualizes the Orthodox understanding of the communion of the saints: that we indeed all worship God together in the dimension of the Kingdom.

PEOPLE: *Amen.*

DEACON (TO THE PRIEST): *Father, bless the entrance of your saints.*

And in anticipation of the entrance into the Kingdom:

PRIEST: *Blessed be the entrance of Your saints, always, now and ever and unto ages of ages. Amen.*

The deacon now offers the Gospel book to the priest, who reverently kisses it.

DEACON: *Wisdom! Let us attend!*

The deacon, followed by the priest, now enters the sanctuary through the Royal Doors and places the Gospel book on the altar. Then are sung the variable hymns of the day. These hymns are called *troparia* and *kontakia*. The *troparia* are short poetic sacred verses inserted between verses of psalms. A somewhat later poetic innovation, less dependent on Scripture than the earlier *troparia* is the form known as *kontakia*, which consists of a variable number of individual stanzas forming a sequence. These *troparia* and *kontakia* are appropriate to the day and are sung in one of eight modes or tones. They are, in essence, special hymns developed in the ancient Eastern tradition, and are vehicles of both praise and instruction. At their conclusion, the priest stands before the altar and recites the prayer of the Trisagion (thrice-holy) Hymn.

The Little Entrance, so called to distinguish it from the Great Entrance that initiates the Eucharistic Liturgy, has been given numerous symbolic explanations. For example, the emergence of the priest and deacon from the sanctuary with the Gospel into the body of the church and their final return with it into the sanctuary have sometimes been likened to the appearance of Jesus Christ on earth, coming from heaven (the sanctuary) into the world (the nave), carrying out His earthly mission, and after His Passion and Resurrection ascending again to the Father. We should recall, however, that at the core of all of these explanations is the historical source we saw in Part I: the bringing of the Gospel and the Gifts, carried by the clergy, and the collective entrance of all into the church. After the singing of the litanies and antiphons the clergy would vest outside the sanctuary and at this point would make entry with the Gospel book into the sanctuary, to the altar, which represents the throne of Christ in the Kingdom. It is significant that this original practice is still followed by the bishop, who vests in the narthex and enters the sanctuary at this time—the true beginning of the Liturgy of the

Word. In many ways it is unfortunate that the original practice is not more closely followed, since the sacramental nature of the coming together of the people, praying together and actualizing the mystical Body of Christ, has become somewhat harder to perceive in our present-day order of service.

Recognizing the historical origin and the arrival of the Gospel—the Word of Life—we can understand the Little Entrance for what it is in the structure of the Divine Liturgy. Here, priest and deacon, as they stand before the Royal Doors, stand at the very threshold of the Kingdom. What happens in these successive stages of the Divine Liturgy is not symbolic but actual. Thus, as the priest advances into the sanctuary through the Royal Doors, he leads the people over the threshold of the Kingdom, stepping literally from this world into the next. And since the whole of the Divine Liturgy is a progression, an ascent (an *anaphora*, to use the technical term), then the clergy and all the people will be lifted up spiritually from the ordinary world into the dimension of the Kingdom of God.

The Little Entrance is the first bold step across that threshold. Thus in the prayer of the Entrance we ask God for His holy angels to enter with us, that both they and we may together glorify His goodness. For soon, in the great Eucharistic Prayer, we shall indeed stand before the Throne, invisibly escorted by the angelic hosts to worship the Divine Majesty and to receive the Bread of Life.

The Trisagion Hymn

We return now to the priest standing at the altar. He reads the prayer of the Trisagion Hymn. This prayer sets the stage for what is to come.

PRIEST: *O Holy God, who rests in the saints, who with the Trisagion Hymn are praised by the seraphim, glorified by the cherubim, and worshiped by the heavenly powers, who out of nothing brought all things into being, who created mankind in Your image and likeness and adorned him with every gift of Your grace, who gives wisdom and understanding to anyone asking for them, and who do not disregard the sinner, but have appointed repentance for salvation, who have made us, Your humble and unworthy servants, even at this hour, to stand before the glory of Your holy altar and to offer You the worship and praise due to You: accept O Lord, from the mouths of us sinners, the Trisagion Hymn and visit us in Your goodness.*

Forgive us every transgression whether voluntary or involuntary. Sanctify our souls and bodies, grant that we may worship You in holiness all the days of our lives, through the intercessions of the holy Theotokos and of all the saints who have pleased You from the beginning. For You are holy, O our God, and to You we ascribe glory, to the Father, to the Son and the Holy Spirit, now and ever ...

DEACON: *... and unto ages of ages.*

PEOPLE: *Amen.*

Then the people sing the Trisagion Hymn:

Holy God, Holy Mighty, Holy Immortal One, have mercy on us. Holy God, Holy Mighty, Holy Immortal One, have mercy on us.

Glory be to the Father, and to the Son, and to the Holy Spirit, now and ever and unto ages of ages, Amen.

Holy Immortal One, have mercy on us.

PRIEST OR DEACON (IN SOME TRADITIONS): *With strength! (Dynamis!)*

PEOPLE (LOUDER): *Holy God, Holy Mighty, Holy Immortal One, have mercy on us.*

This is one of the most ancient hymns of the Christian Church. It is a hymn deeply Trinitarian in character, for those who are addressed in this hymn are none other than the Father, the Son, and the Holy Spirit. *Holy God* is addressed to the Father Almighty, *Holy Mighty* to the only-begotten Son, and *Holy Immortal One* refers in turn to the Holy Spirit, who proceeds from the Father through the Son.

Again, there are the pleas for mercy—that is, for steadfast love and compassion. For as we know, God is love: God is all-compassionate, all-knowing, and all-understanding. The pleas for mercy, therefore, are asking God merely to be Himself to us and to lift us up—who are fashioned in His image—that we may come to know Him and to do His will.

The Epistle Reading

As the glorious petitions of the Trisagion die away, the deacon comes to the Royal Doors.

DEACON: *Wisdom!*

PRIEST: *Peace be to all.*

DEACON: *Let us be attentive!*

The cantor will then sing the *prokeimenon*, which means "that which goes before." The prokeimenon was originally an entire psalm but has now been reduced to a short verse appropriate to the day. For example, on ordinary Sundays the following is sung:

Let Your mercy, O Lord, be upon us, as we have hoped in You (Ps. 31/32:22).

Rejoice in the Lord, O you righteous; praise befits the just.

This is followed by:

DEACON: *Wisdom!*

READER: *The reading from the Epistle of the Holy Apostle (N) to the (N).*

DEACON: *Let us attend!*

Then the epistle appointed for the day is read.

The reading of the Holy Scriptures—Epistle and Gospel—is the very heart of the Liturgy of the Word and traces its origins directly to the synagogue worship of the Jews. The reading of the Epistle is followed by the prescribed Gospel reading for the day.

The Epistles and Gospels proper to each day follow a strict cyclic course in the Eastern tradition. This cycle begins not on the first day of the ecclesiastical year (September 1), but on Easter Sunday, a practice that seems to have been Byzantine in origin and can be traced back to the eighth century. The cycle concludes on Palm Sunday of the following year and is then interrupted by the highly specialized and solemn services of Holy Week. The new cycle begins again on Easter Sunday, as Holy Week is concluded.

It is customary for the people to sit during the reading of the epistle and to listen to the teaching of the apostle. At its conclusion the priest addresses the reader:

PRIEST: *Peace be unto you, the reader.*

PEOPLE: *Alleluia, alleluia, alleluia!*

In many traditions the threefold refrains of Alleluia are antiphonally interspersed with psalm verses, much as with the antiphons.

The Reading of the Gospel

The people are now standing to receive the fullness of the Gospel, the Word of God transmitted to us directly by the evangelists themselves, which brings the Good News directly into our lives, proclaiming it still as it was proclaimed in the beginning. Once again, the Church shows forth its timelessness. The Gospel, proclaimed in time, has transcended time. Each succeeding generation hears it afresh, so that with each generation there is in a sense a new beginning. And so it exists both within the framework of time and throughout eternity, beyond the confines of time or of any other changeable category.

If the deacon is to read the Gospel lesson, he approaches the priest, bows slightly in his direction, and holding his stole lightly in his right hand, indicates the Gospel book.

> DEACON: *Master, bless the one who goes to announce the Gospel of the Holy Apostle and Evangelist (N).*

> PRIEST: *May God, through the prayers of the holy, glorious, and most praiseworthy Apostle and Evangelist (N), grant you the power of announcing His Word with great strength for fulfilling your office of singing the gospel of His well-beloved Son, our Lord Jesus Christ.*

Then the deacon bows slightly towards the Gospel book. He takes the book and, preceded by candle-bearers who pass out of the sanctuary through the north and south doors respectively, he passes through the Royal Doors to stand in the solea, facing the people. The priest stands at the Royal Doors, immediately in front of the altar but facing the people.

> PRIEST: *Wisdom! Let us stand upright! Let us hear the holy Gospel. Peace be to all!*

> PEOPLE: *And to your spirit!*

This declaration by the priest, the icon of Christ, is taken from the very words of Christ when he appeared to the disciples after the Resurrection. Saint John records that Christ appeared to them and said, "Peace to you" (John 20:21). Truly, in preparation for the hearing of the Gospel, the Word of Life, it is the peace of Jesus Christ, which we not only should desire but in fact require. Without this peace, given by the Holy Spirit, how can these words become the Word? And how could we possibly understand them without the ears to hear and the eyes to see (Matt. 13:16)?

DEACON: *The reading is from the Holy Gospel according to Saint (N).*

PEOPLE: *Glory to You, O Lord, glory to You.*

PRIEST: *Let us be attentive!*

The deacon then reads the holy Gospel. If no deacon is present then the Gospel is read by the priest from before the Royal Doors. Whereas a layperson may read the epistle, the Gospel is read by the clergy—deacon or priest. This is in keeping with traditional practice and is a special mark of reverence toward the written Word of God. After the reading of the Gospel:

PRIEST (TO THE DEACON): *Praise be unto you who have announced the Good News.*

PEOPLE: *Glory to You, O Lord, glory to You.*

The deacon returns to the sanctuary through the Royal Doors, handing the Gospel book to the priest, who reverently kisses it and replaces it on the altar.

The presence of the Gospel book on the altar throughout the Divine Liturgy is of great significance. During the celebration of the Eucharist, the altar actualizes the Throne of God in the Kingdom; that is, it shows forth the Holy of Holies. And it is here, directly adjacent to the very Body and Blood of Christ, that the written record of the words spoken by the Incarnate God will be revered and exalted.

According to ancient tradition, nothing that is not essential to the Divine Liturgy—to the Eucharist—should lie upon the Holy Table. In the strict tradition, there should be no flowers, no candlesticks, no superfluous articles of any kind. The seven-branched candelabra should stand behind the altar, sending its radiance down upon it. Only the sacred vessels bearing the gifts and those things essential to the celebration of the Eucharist should be upon the altar, together with the Gospel book. For the Gospel book is a visible and tangible and proclaimed actualization of the Word; it is therefore integral to and inseparable from the Word Himself.

Other marks of special reverence and honor are shown to the Gospel. In all services in which the Gospel is read it is always the last lesson to be read. This special reserving particularly emphasizes the Gospel's incomparable worth and dignity. Placing the most significant thing in the last position is shown forth in the practices of the Church in many ways. For example, in procession the highest-ranking clergy generally walk at the end. Not only does this draw attention to the dignity of the office, rather than to the individual: it also demonstrates the principle that the first shall be last. It is important to emphasize that the dignity of office carries with it the dignity of service to others, which in turn bears the requirement of humility.

Again, when the Gospel book is carried into the solea prior to the reading, it is preceded by candle-bearers. This is a mark of distinction shown especially to the Word of Christ. It should be noted also that all stand during the reading of the Gospel. In announcing the reading, the celebrant chants, "Wisdom! Let us stand upright!" This again emphasizes the profound reverence in which the spoken Word of God is held within the Church.

Moreover, everyone stands bare-headed: even the bishop removes his mitre at this juncture. Likewise, the responses made by the people—"Glory to You, O Lord, glory to You"—which come before and after the Gospel reading, are exclamations of joy at hearing the very Word of God and of reverence and respect for the Word. In hearing the Gospel, we hear the Lord Himself—His words are actualized for us, and in listening to the reading we stand before Him and directly receive His teaching. The actions of the priest and the deacon and the people's interactions with them are not illustrations but realities: we are truly receiving the Word of God, and with it the realization of the Kingdom.

The Homily

From the very earliest times, following the reading of the Gospel there has been a spoken interpretation of the scriptural passage just read. This also follows from early synagogue practice, in which a spoken exposition of the scripture for the day was an integral part of the service. It is thus highly appropriate that the sermon or homily (*omilia* in Greek) should be preached at this time, when the content of the Gospel lesson is fresh in the minds of the people. Moreover, it is one of the earliest of traditions that this homily is a further commentary on the Word of God and should develop the theme of the Gospel reading.

Preaching the Gospel is one of the most fundamental duties of the Christian ministry. Jesus Himself took many opportunities to do this, as, for example, in Nazareth (Mark 6:2–4, Luke 4:16–30). Similarly, Justin Martyr indicates that in the primitive Church, immediately after the reading of the lessons, the celebrant gave a speech exhorting all the people to imitate those things with which the lesson was concerned.[78] Passages in the *Apostolic Constitutions* and the writings of St. Cyprian of Carthage, Tertullian, and St. Clement of Alexandria all make it clear that a homily followed immediately upon the reading of the scriptural lessons. The homily has been used as a vehicle for instruction for almost the entire

---

78 Casimir Kucharek, *The Byzantine-Slav Liturgy of St. John Chrysostom: Its Origin and Evolution* (Allendale, NJ: Alleluia Press, 1970), 42.

life of the Church and has attained to great heights of development at the hands of some outstanding masters. For example, St. John Chrysostom—perhaps the greatest of all Bible expositors—gave addresses on many occasions that may have lasted in excess of two hours. But this length was more than compensated for by the wonder of the content.

The place of the sermon must not be underestimated. It constitutes a teaching function based upon the very word of God, and it is just as much a part of the Liturgy as the reading of the lessons themselves. It is important, however, that the subject matter and content of the sermon correspond to the scriptural lessons and most especially to the Gospel reading. The sermon is not the place for political harangues or for the personal opinions of any person, whether clergy or otherwise. If the sermon loses its exegetical character and degenerates into soapbox oratory, it becomes not only divorced from its primary purpose but also an offense against God and an expression of spiritual pride. In wisdom let us attend, for the lessons taken from the Word of God surpass any ordinary human interpretation.

At one time, at this point in the Divine Liturgy the Litany of Fervent Supplication was performed. The Royal Doors would be closed and the deacon would come out of the sanctuary, stand before the doors, and recite a brief litany, in which certain petitions made in previous litanies would be repeated in an insistent manner. These would include prayers for mercy and prayers for the patriarch and the bishop, the founders of the parish, and those who serve in the Church. In many places this litany has unfortunately fallen out of use. The original intention was to emphasize with fervor and zeal the unity of the Church—the patriarch with the bishop, the bishop with the priest, the priest with the people—as an organic or catholic whole. To each of the petitions of this litany the people responded with the words "Lord, have mercy" three times, stressing the passionate nature of the appeals to God. Fortunately, there is a developing trend in Orthodoxy to restore some of these petitions. An understanding of the liturgical life of the Church would, we believe, create a growing popular demand for the inclusions of such parts.

The Dismissals

In the early Church, on concluding the Litany of Fervent Supplication it was customary to ask to depart from the church those who were yet unbaptized but had attended the Liturgy of the Word in order to receive Christian instruction. At this period, the primary parts of the Liturgy were much more strictly defined. The Liturgy of the Word, which was open to anyone, was intended primarily to teach the people, and therefore those preparing for membership in the Church but not yet received by baptism and chrismation were expected to prayerfully seek instruction from this portion. Since they were not yet members of the Church, the celebration of the Eucharist was at that time closed to them, so sacred was it considered, so reverently and jealously was it guarded. This dismissal of those under instruction was termed the Dismissal of the Catechumens. (Catechumens are those undergoing instruction in the Faith in preparation for baptism and chrismation.)

For a long time, this dismissal of the unbaptized has been discontinued, or rather has been allowed to lapse. The principal reason for this is simply that the number of catechumens had diminished to a very low point, and so in many cases there was no longer anyone to dismiss. With the great resurgence of Orthodoxy that is now beginning, more and more catechumens are once again beginning to appear, a source of great joy to all of us. However, it is most unlikely that anyone will be excluded from any part of the Divine Liturgy in the future. Rather, we send out the message "Come and see!"

More and more people are seeking and finding the fulfillment of their spiritual path in Orthodoxy and are increasingly visiting our churches in their quest for the fullness of spiritual life. Since this will mean renewed instruction in the Faith, the restoration of certain prayers and intercessions on behalf of the catechumens would be highly desirable. Thus the following intercessions, still generally practiced in the Russian church, are recommended for general use:

DEACON: *Catechumens, pray to the Lord.*

PEOPLE: *Lord, have mercy.*

DEACON: *Let us, the faithful, pray for the catechumens, that the Lord have mercy on them.*

PEOPLE: *Lord, have mercy.*

DEACON: *That He instruct them in the word of truth.*

PEOPLE: *Lord, have mercy.*

DEACON: *That He reveal to them the gospel of righteousness.*

PEOPLE: *Lord, have mercy.*

DEACON: *That He unite them to His Holy, Catholic, and Apostolic Church.*

PEOPLE: *Lord, have mercy.*

DEACON: *Save them, have mercy on them, help and protect them, O God, by Your grace.*

PEOPLE: *Lord, have mercy.*

DEACON: *Catechumens, bow your heads unto the Lord.*

PEOPLE: *To You, O Lord.*

PRIEST: *O Lord our God, who dwell on high and watch over the humble, who sent forth as the salvation of the human race your only-begotten Son and God, our Lord Jesus*

Christ, look down upon Your servants, the catechumens, who have bowed their necks before You. Make them worthy in due time of the laver of regeneration, the remission of sins, and the robe of incorruption. Unite them to Your Holy, Catholic, and Apostolic Church, and number them with Your chosen flock, that with us they may glorify Your all honorable and majestic name, of the Father and of the Son and of the Holy Spirit, now and ever and unto ages of ages.

PEOPLE: *Amen.*

The general form of these intercessory prayers has changed little since the fourth century, or even earlier. They need to be present with us again as we open the twenty-first century.

CHAPTER 9

The Liturgy of the Eucharist

W E COME NOW TO THE third and climactic division of the Divine Liturgy, the Liturgy of the Eucharist. This is sometimes called the Liturgy of the Faithful, referring to the fact that at one time only the faithful—baptized and chrismated Orthodox—were permitted to attend it. This title could imply some symbolic ceremony shrouded in secrecy and attended by a privileged group, but in truth, the Eucharist is the most glorious, most joyous, and most elevating event permitted to humanity. It is the Sacrament of the Kingdom of God, our ascent to heaven. It is here where two worlds meet, this world and the world to come. Here we move into the dimension of the Kingdom, where sanctification and salvation become available to us. It is now that we shall feed upon the heavenly food. It is here that we shall celebrate the Feast of the Kingdom. For it is here that we shall show the Lord's death until He comes (1 Cor. 11:26). Let us then move forward into His presence.

The deacon now calls upon the people to pray.

DEACON: *Let us, the faithful, pray to the Lord.*

PEOPLE: *Lord, have mercy.*

PRIEST (THE PRAYER OF THE FAITHFUL): *Often and again we fall down before You and implore You, O gracious*

*Lord, lover of mankind, to regard our prayer and to purify
our souls and bodies from all defilement of flesh and
spirit. And grant that we may stand before Your holy altar
without guile or condemnation. And grant us, O God, and
those praying with us, progress in life, faith, and spiritual
understanding. Grant that they may always worship You
and partake of Your Holy Mysteries with fear and love
and without guilt and condemnation, and that they may
be made worthy of Your heavenly Kingdom.*

DEACON: *Help us, save us, have mercy on us and keep us, O
God, by Your grace.*

PEOPLE: *Lord, have mercy.*

DEACON: *Wisdom!*

PRIEST: *That always being protected by Your power, we may
send up glory to You, to the Father and to the Son and to
the Holy Spirit, now and ever and unto ages of ages.*

PEOPLE: *Amen.*

The deacon calls upon the faithful to pray to the Lord. Originally,
only the faithful remained in the church at this time, the catechumens having been dismissed. It is a call to prayer and devotion,
to be conducted in an atmosphere of peace, the peace that was
asked for in the very first petitions of the Great Litany. Whatever
divisions existed between persons, whatever cares or anxieties
they may have had before this time, all must now be laid aside
and the concerns of this world be left behind. The Prayer of the
Faithful, recited by the celebrating priest, contains insistent and
urgent pleas for all the people. "We . . . implore You . . . to regard
our prayer." This is sometimes rendered "regard our entreaty" or
"regard our plea." It derives from the speech made by Solomon
at the solemn dedication of his temple (1 Kin. 8:28). It is most

appropriate here, for it seeks God's mercy and blessing upon the assembled people within the Church, the temple of the New Covenant.

The priest also prays "for us, and those praying with us, progress in life, faith, and spiritual understanding." The priest stands before God on behalf of himself and the people, making no difference or distinction between them. He thus shows forth the unity and solidarity of the community—clergy and laity alike—as the people of God. The words of the prayer are of great significance, for they ask God, in essence, to create in His people by grace the ardent desire, the fervent and spiritual dedication, to make the eucharistic sacrifice acceptable to Him. Truly, that which is offered in the Divine Liturgy—Christ Himself actualized in the Eucharist—is of infinite, immeasurable, and inconceivable worth and is thus infinitely pleasing to God.

On the other hand, the gift of sacramental grace that the people (clergy and laity together) derive will bear close relationship to the dedication and sincerity of their offering. That this is so is clear from the words of St. Paul:

> Therefore whoever eats this bread or drinks *this* cup of the Lord in an unworthy manner will be guilty of the body and blood of the Lord. But let a man examine himself, and so let him eat of the bread and drink of the cup. For he who eats and drinks in an unworthy manner eats and drinks judgment to himself, not discerning the Lord's body. (1 Cor. 11:27–29)

And reminiscent of St. Paul's admonition, the prayer petitions that all may partake of the Mysteries, the Eucharist, without guilt or condemnation and with reverence and love. In such a spirit, we may hope always to be protected by the divine power and to render thanks and glory to Him from whom all that we are and all that we possess—including our very existence—is derived.

There is also the immediate plea to God to cleanse and purify our souls and bodies and to rid them of every defilement. This echoes a similar plea of St. Paul to the Christian community in Corinth, which was in turmoil, that they do the same and so become more worthy of receiving the Mysteries (2 Cor. 7:11). In the ancient Eastern church the notion that sin—or at least certain sins—could defile the whole person, body and soul, was widely held and undoubtedly derived from the earlier Jewish concept of both spiritual and bodily defilement. In ancient Judaism, as the Scriptures teach, certain sins brought about not only spiritual defilement but uncleanness of the body. Ritual purification—cleansing of the body by ceremonial washing—was required to remove the sin and to render the person acceptable to perform religious offices or attend religious functions. It seems clear that a similar concept carried forward into the Christian tradition, but in this case the cleansing of the soul and the body could be accomplished by direct appeal to God, as in the case of this intercessory prayer.

The Cherubic Hymn and the Great Entrance

After completing the intercessory prayers, to which the people respond "Amen," the priest recites the prayer of the Cherubic Hymn:

> PRIEST: *No one bound by fleshly desires and pleasures is worthy to approach or come near or minister before You, the King of Glory. For to serve You is great and awesome, even to the heavenly powers themselves. Yet because of Your unspeakable and immeasurable love for mankind, You became man without undergoing change or alteration. And being called our High Priest, You, as Lord of all, have committed to us the celebration of this liturgical and unbloody sacrifice. For You alone, O Lord our God,*

rule over all things in heaven and earth, You who are seated upon the throne of the cherubim and are Lord of the seraphim and King of Israel, who alone are holy and rest in the saints. Therefore I implore You, who alone are good and ready to hear: look upon me, Your sinful and unprofitable servant, and cleanse my soul and heart from an evil conscience. And enable me by the power of Your Holy Spirit, clothed with the grace of the priesthood, to stand before this Your holy table, and to consecrate Your holy and spotless Body and precious Blood. For to You I come bowing my neck, and I pray to You: do not turn away Your face from me, nor reject me from among Your children, but make me, Your sinful and unworthy servant, worthy to offer these gifts to You. For You alone are the Offeror and the Offered, the Receiver and the Distributed, O Christ our God, and we send up glory to You, together with Your Father who is without beginning, and Your all-holy, good, and life-giving Spirit, now and ever and unto ages of ages. Amen.

As this prayer is recited, the choir and the people sing together the first part of the Cherubic Hymn:

Let us who mystically represent the cherubim, and who sing the Trisagion Hymn before the life-creating Trinity, lay aside all earthly cares.

At this point, the priest and deacon go to the preparation table, where the priest takes the censer and censes the Gifts.

PRIEST: *O God, be merciful to me, a sinner.*

Then the priest hands the censer to the deacon.

DEACON: *Take, sir.*

The priest then removes the large veil and places it on the deacon's left shoulder.

PRIEST: *Lift up your hands unto holy places and bless the Lord!*

The priest now takes the paten—the plate holding the bread particles, which is covered with a small veil—and hands it to the deacon. The priest himself then takes the chalice, covered with its small veil, and holds it before his breast. Then, preceded by acolytes carrying candles, they leave the sanctuary by the north door. This begins the Great Entrance, the procession through the church to the altar. In some traditions, the procession includes two cherubic fans, which are carried behind the clergy. These are representations of the cherubim above the altar. As he goes forth the deacon says:

DEACON: *May the Lord our God remember all of us in His Kingdom, always, now and ever and unto ages of ages.*

PEOPLE: *Amen.*

The priest and deacon, preceded by acolytes, now make procession around the church, reciting prayers for the clergy, for the president and those in civil authority, and for the living and the departed. At the completion of these prayers, the choir and people complete the Cherubic Hymn:

CHOIR AND PEOPLE: *That we may receive the King of all, invisibly attended by the angelic hosts. Alleluia! Alleluia! Alleluia!*

These parts of the Liturgy—the Cherubic Hymn and the Great Entrance—are so intimately connected that they must be considered together. Originally, about the ninth century, the Cherubic Hymn was a solemn part of the procession of the Great Entrance, but as we have seen, it is now sung in two parts, one before the entrance and the other immediately after it, at the completion of the priest's commemorations.

When this hymn was first introduced into the Divine Liturgy, it caused considerable controversy. This was particularly true of some monastic communities, who not surprisingly asked how it was possible for human beings to mystically represent the cherubim. The answer to the monks' question is perhaps not so difficult. At the Great Entrance, the Holy Gifts are brought into the church and then are returned to the altar. We witness here the impending entrance of the King of Kings, the Almighty Lord. If we could but perceive these events with pure heart and pure senses, we would behold the Lord of Hosts approaching His Throne, surrounded by hosts of angels and archangels, singing the Thrice-Holy Hymn to the glory of the undivided Trinity (see Isaiah 6 and Revelation 5). In our present mortal circumstances, this is not possible to us; nevertheless, the hymn calls us to lay aside all earthly cares and to enter the presence of the Lord of Hosts, as do the angelic hosts themselves.

It is often taught that we are reminded by the Great Entrance of the entry of Jesus Christ into Jerusalem on Palm Sunday. On this occasion, He was greeted by hosts of citizens bearing palm fronds, who came forth from the city gates and strewed the palms in the path of the donkey upon which He rode, chanting, "Blessed is He who comes in the name of the Lord. Hosanna in the highest." Since the Great Entrance precedes the unbloody sacrifice of the Eucharist, this historical symbolism can be admitted. But it is too simplistic: here we perceive not merely the entry of the Lord of Hosts into Jerusalem as a symbolic reenactment of a past event, but rather we perceive the eschatological fulfillment of the Kingdom—the Lord of Hosts entering upon His glorious Throne in the actualized and eternal Kingdom.

As with the case of the Little Entrance, simple symbolic explanations of these liturgical events are insufficient and inadequate.

We are now moving to the dimension of the Kingdom itself. The events in ancient Jerusalem are past. They occurred but once and may not be repeated. The events of the Divine Liturgy transcend all time; for a moment our temporal world, subject as it is to change and decay, is able to approach and delicately touch that world that is beyond time and space, where change and decay have no longer any place and where death and corruption are no more.

Earlier it was noted that in the Rite of Preparation of the early Church the people brought their donations, from which were selected the gifts, the bread and wine to be used in the Eucharist. These gifts would be brought into the church, brought by the priest into the solea, and from there carried into the sanctuary—the Great Entrance. In modern times the symbolism of this action is captured by the procession of the priest and deacons around the nave, through the congregation, and into the sanctuary. This symbolizes the offering of the gifts and sacrifices of the people, their participation in the one great sacrifice of Jesus Christ, about to be actualized in the Eucharist. The people make the bread, they bring it to the church, their role is clear: all must participate in this offering and sacrifice. All must participate in the singing of the hymn, must lay aside all earthly distractions, and enter like the angelic host into the reality of the divine presence.

The priest now enters the sanctuary through the Royal Doors and places the chalice upon the altar. He then takes the paten from the deacon and places it on the altar to the left of the chalice. Then he removes the veils from the paten and the chalice and places them to one side. Taking the large veil from the deacon, he then censes it by holding it above the censer, then lays it over the Holy Gifts, covering them.

PRIEST: *The noble Joseph, taking Your most pure body from the cross, wrapped it in clean linen and spices and laid it in a new tomb.*

In the grave with Your body but in hell with Your soul as God, in paradise with the thief and on the throne with the Father and the Spirit, O Christ, You are unbound and fill all things.

Because it gives life, because it is more beautiful than paradise itself, Your tomb is more radiant than any royal chamber, O Christ. It is the fountain from which springs our resurrection.

He then takes the censer from the deacon and censes the Holy Gifts three times, saying:

Then shall they offer bulls on Your altar (Psalm 50).

The priest then returns the censer to the deacon, who replaces it on its stand. The deacon now bows to the priest, leaves the sanctuary through the north door, takes his place before the Royal Doors, and begins the next part of the Liturgy. as follows:

The Offering of the Gifts

The Offertory Prayer begins with:

DEACON: *For the precious Gifts that have been offered, let us pray to the Lord.*

PEOPLE: *Lord have mercy.*

The deacon then leads the congregation in a litany much like the Great Litany. It begins with the deacon saying: "Let us complete our prayer to the Lord. For the precious Gifts that have been offered let us pray to the Lord," to which the people respond: "Lord, have mercy."

This second series of petitions is more wide-ranging: for special blessings upon the day, for the help and protection of our guardian angels, for the forgiveness of our transgressions, for all things that are profitable to our souls, for peace, for the grace of repentance, for a Christian end to our life, and for a worthy defense before the judgment seat of Christ. To each of these petitions the people respond: "Grant this, O Lord." These petitions are eschatological (dealing with our ultimate destiny): they address the problems of our present situation, which may well determine the final disposition of our existence. For this reason, we ask God directly to grant them, to accomplish them for us, and to lift us out of the morass we have created for ourselves and into the peace and safety of the Kingdom.

The litany ends with:

PRIEST: *O Lord God, Ruler of all, who alone are holy, who accepts a sacrifice of praise from those who call upon You with all their heart, receive also the prayer of us sinners, and bring us to Your holy Altar. And make us worthy to offer You gifts and spiritual sacrifices for sins and for the errors of Your people. And grant us to find grace in Your eyes, so that our sacrifice may be acceptable to You, and that the good Spirit of Your grace may rest on us and all Your people and on these gifts set before You.*

Through the mercies of Your only-begotten Son, with whom You are blessed, together with Your all-holy and good and life-giving Spirit, now and ever and unto ages of ages.

PEOPLE: *Amen.*

By these petitions and prayers the offering—that is, the presentation of the Holy Gifts prior to the unbloody sacrifice of the Eucharist—is completed. Once again, it is a co-celebration by all persons present: priest, deacon, and people celebrate together as equal members of the royal priesthood. The Gifts have been borne into the sanctuary in advance of the anaphora, that is, before the ascent to heaven begins. *Anaphora* is a word that signifies elevation, not only of the Gifts but also of the assembled Church, constituted by its members, to the heavenly sanctuary. The entry with the Gifts and their presentation upon the altar, followed by the Prayer and the Litany of Offering, completes the succession of that which began in the Rite of Preparation, in which the Gifts were prepared following their being offered by the people.

The Kiss of Peace

Following the completion of the prayer that concludes the Offertory, the priest turns to the people.

PRIEST: *Peace be to all.*

PEOPLE: *And with your spirit.*

Again, we hear the proclamation of these words that Christ Himself said to the disciples (John 20:21). And in anticipation of the Kiss of Peace, we recognize anew how much we are in need of the peace of Jesus Christ. It is into His peace that passes understanding and into the spirit of the Beatitudes that we now must place ourselves, in order that we not presume to approach the Throne of God with any guile, hatred, impurity of heart, doubt, or despair. We must be reconciled one to another. We must be one body in Christ without difference or distinction between us. We must be family: brothers, sisters, fathers, mothers, united in love and peace. This we express tangibly, lovingly, by exchanging the Kiss of Peace.

DEACON: *Let us love one another, that with one accord we may confess:*

PEOPLE: *Father, Son, and Holy Spirit, the consubstantial and undivided Trinity.*

The priest, facing the altar, bows three times and reverently kisses the Holy Gifts, which are covered with their veils.

PRIEST (SILENTLY): *I will love you, Lord, my strength: the Lord is my might and my refuge.*

(TO THE PEOPLE): *Christ is in our midst.*

PEOPLE: *He is and shall be.*

> The priest and deacon now exchange the Kiss of Peace by a small embrace, and following ancient custom the people now exchange the Kiss of Peace with one another, saying:

Christ is in our midst—He is and will be!

Here we express tangibly and lovingly the reconciliation that is ours in Jesus Christ. All are reconciled. All is at peace. All is now ready for the great approach to the Throne.

The Creed: The Symbol of Faith

The deacon now makes three small bows, kisses the image of the Cross that is embroidered on his stole, and chants:

DEACON: *The doors! The doors! In wisdom let us attend!*

This phrase hearkens back to the early times of persecution, when at this point the doors to the church were shut and locked to keep out all who were not believers and who might betray the Church.

The clergy and people now together recite the Nicene Creed, as follows (this is a translation of the Creed from Greek into modern English):

> *I believe in one God, the Father almighty, maker of heaven and earth and of all things visible and invisible. And in one Lord Jesus Christ, the only-begotten Son of God, begotten of the Father before all ages. Light from light, true God from true God, begotten, not created, consubstantial with the Father, through whom all things were made. Who for us humans, and for our salvation, came*

*down from heaven and was incarnate of the Holy Spirit
and the Virgin Mary and became human. Crucified also
for us by Pontius Pilate, He suffered and was buried. And
was resurrected on the third day, in accordance with the
scriptures. And ascended to heaven, and sits at the right
hand of the Father. And He shall come again with glory
to judge the living and dead, whose Kingdom shall have
no end. And in the Holy Spirit, the Lord, the Giver of
Life, who proceeds from the Father, who together with the
Father and the Son is worshiped and glorified, who spoke
through the prophets. And in one holy, catholic, and apostolic Church. I acknowledge one baptism for the remission
of sins. I await the resurrection of the dead and the life of
the age to come. Amen.*

During the recitation of the Nicene Creed, the priest lifts up the
large veil and holds it extended over the Holy Gifts, waving it
with a fanning or vibrating motion as the words are recited. On
completion of the recitation, the veil is folded, reverently kissed
by the priest, then laid to one side on the altar. This action is to
symbolize the rolling away of the stone from the tomb, by which
Jesus rose from the grave unto life—just as the removal of the veil
from the Gifts allows us access to new life by receiving the Body
and Blood of Jesus Christ.

The Nicene Creed, frequently known as the Symbol of Faith, is
a summary statement of the principal tenets of the Holy Orthodox Faith. It grew out of the compelling need to define very clearly
the chief doctrines of belief, which were in turn based on both
Holy Scripture and Holy Tradition, derived directly from Christ
and the apostles and illumined by the Holy Spirit. In the early
centuries, numerous heresies concerning the nature and divinity
of Jesus Christ, the Holy Spirit, and the relationship of the three
Persons of the Holy Trinity had arisen. The Church, guided by
the Holy Spirit, had to take a firm stand on each of these in turn,

which it did by convening the seven ecumenical councils between the fourth and eighth centuries.

The first of these councils, at Nicea in Asia Minor, was convened at the request of the Emperor Constantine in AD 325. The principal concern of this council was the refutation of the Arian heresy, which taught that Jesus Christ was not truly divine but a creature like us, subject to change and therefore not consubstantial with the Father. The Arian heresy was denounced by the Council of Nicea, which formulated a profession of faith known as the Nicene Creed. This creed confined itself primarily to the relationship between the Father and Son and to the nature of the Son. The articles describing the Holy Spirit, the catholic and apostolic Church, and the eschaton (last things), were formulated at the Second Ecumenical Council, held at Constantinople in AD 381.

The result is the Nicene/Constantinopolitan Creed, commonly referred to simply as the Nicene Creed. It represents the basic structure of belief that the early Church Fathers pronounced must be believed by Christians to be canonical members of the Church, and which could not be modified.

CHAPTER 10

The Great Anaphora

A<small>S WE HAVE SEEN, THE</small> word *anaphora* means "elevation" or "lifting up." We now approach this elevation—of the Gifts and of ourselves into the realm of the Kingdom, that there, by the working of the Holy Spirit, we may commune of the Mysteries of Jesus Christ.

D<small>EACON</small>: *Let us stand straight; let us stand with fear; let us attend that we may offer the holy offering in peace.*

P<small>EOPLE</small>: *An offering of peace, a sacrifice of praise.*

The deacon then makes a small bow and enters the sanctuary through the south door, taking his place by the right side of the priest. The priest now turns and blesses the people.

P<small>RIEST</small>: *The grace of our Lord Jesus Christ, and the love of God the Father, and the communion of the Holy Spirit, be with you all!*

P<small>EOPLE</small>: *And with your spirit!*

The priest now turns slowly to face the altar, raises his arms, and intones in a loud voice:

P<small>RIEST</small>: *Let us lift up our hearts!*

PEOPLE: *We lift them up unto the Lord.*

PRIEST: *Let us give thanks unto the Lord.*

PEOPLE: *It is fitting and right to worship the Father, Son, and Holy Spirit, the Trinity, one in essence and undivided.*

We are now within the dimension of the Kingdom and stand at the very threshold of the throne room. For this reason, the deacon exhorts all the people to stand reverently and with the fear of God—that is, stand with some awareness of the incomprehensible immensity of what we are about to experience and of the infinite love of God for His creation. As the short dialogue ends, the priest begins the opening prayer of the Great Anaphora. Read these prayers slowly and with understanding, for here is everything that a person could want to say in response to God's love and mercy.

PRIEST: *It is fitting and right to sing to You, to bless You, to praise You, to give thanks to You, to worship You in every place of Your dominion, for You are God, beyond description, beyond understanding, invisible, incomprehensible, always existing, always the same; You and Your only-begotten Son and Your Holy Spirit. Out of nothing you have brought us into being, and when we had fallen raised us up again, and You have not ceased doing everything until You brought us to heaven and graciously gave us Your future Kingdom. For all these things, we thank You and Your only-begotten Son and Your Holy Spirit; for all that we know and do not know, for the open and hidden benefits bestowed upon us.*

We thank You also for this Liturgy which You are pleased to accept from our hands, though there stand before You thousands of archangels and myriads of angels, cherubim and seraphim, six-winged and many-eyed, soaring high

on their wings, singing, proclaiming, shouting the hymn of
victory.

PEOPLE: *Holy! Holy! Holy! Lord of Hosts! Heaven and earth
are filled with Your glory! Hosanna in the highest! Blessed
is He who comes in the Name of the Lord! Hosanna in the
highest!*

Facing the altar, the priest now begins the Eucharistic
Prayer:

PRIEST: *With these blessed powers, O Lord who loves mankind, we also cry aloud and say: You are holy, most holy.
You and Your only-begotten Son and Your Holy Spirit.
You are holy, most holy, and magnificent is Your glory.
You have so loved the world that You gave Your only-
begotten Son, that whoever believes in Him should not
perish but have everlasting life. And after He had come
and accomplished all that was appointed, on the night
in which He was given up, or rather gave Himself up for
the life of the world, took bread in His holy, most pure,
and blameless hands, and when He had given thanks and
blessed and sanctified and broken it, He gave it to His holy
disciples and apostles, saying: "Take. Eat. This is My body
which is broken for you for the remission of sins."*

PEOPLE: *Amen.*

PRIEST: *And likewise, after supper, He took the cup, saying:
"Drink from it all of you. This is My blood of the New
Testament, which is shed for you and for many, for the
remission of sins."*

PEOPLE: *Amen.*

These are the words of institution—the words by which Jesus
Christ, the Incarnate Word, *instituted* the Sacrament of Holy

Eucharist at the Last Supper. During their recitation, the people properly remain standing, their hearts at peace, their thoughts locked upon the Mystery of which they themselves are a part. By their "Amen" (so be it), they affirm that which their Lord declared, that in His Body and Blood is forgiveness of sins and eternal life.

> PRIEST: *Remembering this saving commandment and all that has been done for us, the cross, the tomb, the resurrection on the third day, the ascension into heaven, the sitting at the right hand, and the second and glorious coming, we offer You Your own, from what is Your own, for everyone and for everything.*

While the priest is saying this, the deacon takes the paten in his right hand, and with his left he picks up the chalice. He then elevates the sacred vessels, making the sign of the cross with them over the altar. When the priest finishes, the people respond:

> PEOPLE: *We praise You, we bless You, we give thanks to You, O Lord, and we pray unto You, our God.*

When, at the Last Supper, Christ accomplished the transformation of the bread and wine into His Body and Blood, He reminded His apostles that whenever in the future they were to do these things—that is to celebrate the Holy Eucharist—they would do so in remembrance of Him. Some people sadly misinterpret this injunction of Christ, confining it merely to the events of the Lord's Supper itself, and somehow deriving from the words as usually presented in English translations a meaning that future generations were merely to mentally remember those particular events. In such an interpretation, the Holy Eucharist would have no significance except as some kind of stylized memorial of the historic Jesus, and the sacramentality of the event would be lost.

As we noted earlier, it was not merely a symbolic gesture that the Lord performed at the Last Supper in Jerusalem. On the contrary, it was the institution of the very event toward which all the other events are ultimately directed, the event that was to project and provide the saving grace of the Body and Blood of the Lord Jesus for all generations, even to the end of the world. There can be no doubt of its significance. Recall the words of Christ to the apostles: "I am the living bread which came down from heaven. If anyone eats of this bread, he will live forever; and the bread that I shall give is My flesh, which I shall give for the life of the world" (John 6:51).

As we have already seen, St. Paul instructs us to celebrate the Lord's Supper in the manner that he himself received from the Lord. We are told to "do these things in remembrance of Me." To do these things in remembrance simply means that we should continue to do them as the Lord Himself did them. The word *remembrance* is an English rendering of the Greek *anamnesis*—a noun that is difficult to translate accurately since it denotes not a single occurrence but a process. Whereas "remembrance" is close, in the New Testament context the word conveys the idea of action—"remembering, recollecting, calling forth again"—and it is this sense that the Church has always understood its usage. As the Church understands it, the word implies the continued actualization of an event first celebrated at the Last Supper, and continuing to be celebrated in the context of the Kingdom, as a main event of salvation. This is why St. Justin Martyr was careful to use the word *anamniskomen* when referring to the Eucharistic Liturgy but used a quite different term when he described the Gospels as memorials of Christ (*genomeno*).[79] Moreover, in remembering the central event of the Eucharist, the word used is *anamnesis*—the continued bringing before us of the great Mystery of salvation.

The words spoken at the Little Elevation over the chalice and paten are sometimes a little difficult to interpret. "Your own of

---

79 Kucharek, 44.

Your own we offer unto You, on behalf of all and for all (things)." The Holy Eucharist is offered on behalf of all creation, just as Christ became incarnate to make possible the redemption of all creation. It is Christ who really offers and is at the same time offered. Everything that exists belongs to God, including ourselves and our very being. Were we but for a fleeting moment outside of God's loving care, we would disappear instantly into nothingness and oblivion.

Therefore, in our great *eucharistia*—thanksgiving—we can only offer to God those things that belong already to His creation and that are His. And we offer them on behalf of all created beings and in thanksgiving for His creation and all that it embraces, in which we ourselves have our being and of which we ourselves are a part. The priest with great reverence now begins the invocation of the Holy Spirit. Technically, this is known as the *epiklesis*—a word that means "calling upon," "calling forth," or "calling down upon." The prayer is addressed to the Father.

> PRIEST: *Again we offer unto You this spiritual and unbloody worship, and beseech You and pray You and supplicate You: send down Your Holy Spirit upon us and upon these Gifts here presented.*

In this prayer, we acknowledge the one sacrifice of Jesus Christ on the Cross for our salvation. (Our sacrifice here is unbloody because we are not re-sacrificing; rather, we are participating in that eternal sacrifice.) And so we pray for the descent of the Holy Spirit upon the people also, for there are no incantations here. The transformation of the bread and wine is not magic: it is due to the mysterious working of the Holy Spirit in both the Gifts and in the people. Having said this prayer, the priest signs the bread and the chalice with the sign of the Cross.

> PRIEST: *And this bread the Precious Body of Your Christ.*

DEACON AND PEOPLE: *Amen.*

PRIEST: *And that which is in this cup, the Precious Blood of Your Christ.*

DEACON AND PEOPLE: *Amen.*

PRIEST: *Changing them by Your Holy Spirit.*

DEACON AND PEOPLE: *Amen! Amen! Amen!*

In the Orthodox Faith, as we saw in Part I, the changing of the ordinary bread and wine into the Body and Blood of Jesus Christ is accomplished by the Holy Spirit in the context of the Kingdom and involves the priest and people exercising their royal priesthood. We recognize that here is a great mystery. But we also recognize that this manifestation of the Body and Blood of Christ takes place not within our ordinary dimensions of space and time, nor in the context of this fallen and changeable world. Rather, it takes place in the eternal, eschatological dimension of the Kingdom of God, to which we ascend spiritually during the Eucharistic Liturgy.

Such a change can take place *only* within the context of the Kingdom, not in a fallen world. At this point in the Divine Liturgy, the two worlds touch—and we are for a brief time spiritually elevated (not symbolically but actually) to the very throne of God, where the transformation of the Gifts can truly take place. This is accomplished by the Holy Spirit: not as an automatic result of saying of a magic formula, but by the prayer of Christ Himself, united to His mystical Body, the Church. All of the members of Christ are praying with Him and within the all-encompassing power of His grace.

It is through the *epiklesis* that the Holy Spirit is invoked upon us *and* upon the Gifts, manifesting the Gifts as the precious Body and Blood. It has always been Orthodox teaching that this invocation of the Holy Spirit is necessary and essential for the manifestation, which is accomplished as a result of the invocation of the Spirit, rather than by the words of institution. The Holy Spirit, who came upon the great day of Pentecost to initiate the Kingdom and the age to come, carries us beyond the present realm and into the heavens. It is the Spirit who transforms the Church into the Mystical Body of Christ and shows forth the simple gifts that make up our offering in the Eucharist as a true communion with Christ in the Holy Spirit. This is what we mean by *consecration*—it is a function of the Spirit working within the Kingdom of God that is wrought for us through the Mystical Body of Christ.

Traditionally, the people stand during the consecration—bowing their heads in great reverence, but nonetheless standing rather than kneeling. Standing reflects the joy, the incalculable happiness of the realization of the divine presence. At this moment our hearts are rejoicing and our spirits are united with Christ in the Mystical Body. We are indeed in heaven.

The priest bows low before the altar.

PRIEST: *That to those who partake of these Gifts, they may be for the cleansing of soul, for the remission of sins, for the communion with Your Holy Spirit, for the fullness of the kingdom of heaven, for freedom in prayer toward You, and not for judgment or for condemnation. Furthermore we offer to you this spiritual worship for those who in faith have gone on before us to their rest: forefathers, fathers, patriarchs, prophets, apostles, preachers, evangelists, martyrs, confessors, ascetics, and every righteous spirit made perfect in faith, especially for our most holy, most pure, most blessed and glorious lady, the Mother of God and Ever-Virgin Mary.*

The people now sing the following hymn of praise to the Theotokos:

166

PEOPLE: *It is truly right to bless you. O Theotokos, ever-blessed and most pure, and the Mother of our God. More honorable than the cherubim and more glorious beyond compare than the seraphim, without defilement you gave birth to God the Word. True Theotokos, we magnify you.*

The priest continues the prayers at the altar, remembering the holy prophet, forerunner, and Baptist John, the apostles, the saint whose memory is commemorated that day, all the saints, and those who have fallen asleep before us in the hope of the resurrection to life eternal. He prays for the bishop, the other clergy, the faithful, and the Church as a whole.

In this sequence of intercessory prayers the assembly of the faithful commemorates in a most distinctive way the Church triumphant. This is the Church of the Kingdom, where the blessed are gathered with the angelic hosts about the Throne.

The reality is that now, after the *epiklesis,* the temporal has truly met the eternal, in that prayers and petitions have been offered before the Gifts—that is, before the Throne of God. It is here that the Church experiences and knows its own totality. The Church militant is the Church in the world, battling to realize the Kingdom. The Church triumphant is in the Kingdom, where it is fully realized. These two expressions of the Church do not exist as separate parts of a single whole. Here, at the eucharistic consecration, they come into full and open contact.

As time passed, the Church realized the true scope of this experience and began to express it in additional prayers and petitions within the Liturgy of the Faithful. These prayers beseech God to remember not only those dwelling on the earth in our vulnerable human condition but also all those who have gone on before us, those who have successfully run the race and have entered the Kingdom. It is for these too, not just ourselves, that the Holy Eucharist, this reasonable worship (or perhaps better, "worship of the Word," as the Greek text states), is offered.

In prayers such as these that immediately follow the *epiklesis* and which commemorate the Church triumphant, we see a shining example of the communion of the saints in action. Here we offer the Eucharist on behalf of the blessed saints and for the blessed Theotokos. Elsewhere and frequently throughout the Divine Liturgy we ask for their intercessions on our behalf. Prayer and petition in the Church are reciprocal, and so the commemoration of the Theotokos and the saints is followed by similar remembrances for the living and the dead and concludes with this prayer:

> PRIEST: *And grant us with one mouth and one heart to glorify and praise Your all-honorable and majestic name: of the Father and of the Son and of the Holy Spirit, now and ever and unto ages of ages.*

> PEOPLE: *Amen.*

> PRIEST (TO THE PEOPLE): *May the mercies of our Great God and Savior Jesus Christ be with you all.*

> PEOPLE: *And with your spirit.*

The Lord's Prayer

We now pass on to the culmination of the Divine Liturgy, the offering and reception of Holy Communion. In some traditions, the Communion rite begins with another litany, much like the Great Litany that began the Divine Liturgy. Frequently, though, it is shortened as follows:

> PRIEST: *Having remembered all the saints, again and again in peace let us pray to the Lord.*

> PEOPLE: *Lord, have mercy.*

> PRIEST: *For the precious Gifts that have been offered and*

sanctified, let us pray to the Lord.

PEOPLE: *Lord, have mercy.*

PRIEST: *That our loving God who has received them upon His holy, heavenly, and spiritual altar, as an offering of spiritual fragrance, may in return send down upon us divine grace and the gift of the Holy Spirit, let us pray to the Lord.*

PEOPLE: *Lord, have mercy.*

PRIEST: *Help us, save us, have mercy on us, and keep us, O God, by Your grace.*

PEOPLE: *Lord, have mercy.*

PRIEST: *Having prayed for the unity of the Faith, and for the communion of the Holy Spirit, let us commit ourselves and each other and our whole life to Christ our God.*

PEOPLE: *To You, O Lord.*

These prayers constitute the final preparation of the faithful, who collectively come before God and offer up the specific requests that are contained in the Lord's Prayer. In this final litany we not only thank God once again but acknowledge that what we are about to receive in Holy Communion is entirely of Him, a manifestation of His grace. We pray to experience His divine grace and Holy Spirit that we may be nurtured and strengthened to lead spiritual lives.

PRIEST: *And make us worthy, O Lord, that with boldness and without condemnation we may dare to call upon You, the heavenly God, as Father and say:*

ALL: *Our Father, who are in heaven, hallowed be Your Name; Your Kingdom come, Your will be done, on earth as it is in heaven. Give us this day our daily bread, and forgive us our debts as we forgive our debtors. And lead us not into temptation, but deliver us from evil.*

PRIEST: *For Thine is the kingdom, the power, and the glory, of the Father and of the Son and of the Holy Spirit, now and ever and unto ages of ages.*

PEOPLE: *Amen.*

From relatively informal beginnings in the very first centuries, the prayers before Holy Communion rapidly became crystallized in the years that followed the Council of Nicea. This was particularly true in Jerusalem and Antioch, where great emphasis was placed in the very early times on the immeasurable sanctity of the Body and Blood of Christ and the awesome character of receiving the Sacrament itself. In keeping with this, therefore, these preparatory prayers were added, probably during the course of the fourth century. By the latter part of that century the Lord's Prayer had been included, first at Jerusalem, then at Antioch, and soon thereafter through all the churches of Christendom. The Lord's Prayer is the quintessential prayer of all Christianity; it is a prayer from which many other prayers of the Church are derived, either directly or indirectly, and which in itself contains the essence of the message of the Faith and guidance for salvation.

The Lord's Prayer is not a general prayer offered for recitation by the whole of mankind. When Christ taught it, He did so only to His immediate disciples, and that in direct response to their plea "Lord, teach us to pray" (Luke 11:1–4). Two observations about the Lord's Prayer are illustrative of its relevance in the Divine Liturgy.

It is highly significant that throughout the Gospels Jesus Christ frequently uses two expressions that are totally unique to Himself. First, He uses the word *Amen* (let it be so) before rather than after making a definite statement. Thus, "Amen, Amen I say unto

170

you" means "Let what I say be so" or "What I say shall be so." This underscores His Lordship, His absolute authority. In addition, He refers to the supra-heavenly God, God the Father, as "My Father." Always, in referring to the Father, this familiar "My" is used, thus identifying Himself in a fully filial relationship to the Godhead. No one anywhere else in Holy Scripture takes such liberty.

Yet in the Lord's Prayer He extends to us fallen creatures the incomparable and unique privilege of addressing as Father the divine majesty of the Lord of all, the God of Abraham, Isaac, and Jacob, the Creator and Ruler of the cosmos, He who is and ever shall be. And not only as Father, but *Abba*, an Aramaic diminutive term perhaps best translated as "dad," "daddy," or "papa." This is the God who created and rules, the God who is not just heavenly but is beyond all things. The Greek word is *epouranion*, supra-heavenly, reminding us that God is beyond the heavenlies. He transcends all that we know and can conceive, and we can approach Him on His terms alone. Note the words of the Liturgy that immediately precede the prayer:

PRIEST: *Grant, O Lord, that with boldness and without condemnation we may dare to call upon You, the supra-heavenly God, as Father and to say . . .*

We dare to call the Lord of all "Father," even as we would address our own parent. Note that in the prayer, Jesus tells us to address God as "our Father." We are never told to address Him as "my Father." That degree of possessiveness is reserved entirely to the Son of God, Jesus Christ, who is His Son from all eternity by nature. Yet we as human beings may become by the operation of divine grace what Christ is by nature. Thus, we too may become children of God and brothers and sisters of Christ by adoption through His infinite mercy and love in the Holy Spirit. And since we belong one to another, all partake equally and uniformly of our human nature. We do so collectively and never as individuals, and thus we must address the living God as "our Father" and never in an individual or possessive way.

The second observation concerns the petition "Give us this day our *daily* bread." In the St. Matthew text, the Greek word translated as *daily* does not in fact mean "daily." The word is *epiousion*, a word that really means "supra-substantial" or "supra-essential" and is thus mysterious to understand. Opinions among the Fathers of the Church as well as among more recent commentators on the New Testament have differed on the meaning of this word. However, much of the evidence points to a translation of the word in terms of the imperishable bread which is Christ Himself and which continues to be available to us in the Holy Eucharist. Note the words of Jesus Himself:

> Then Jesus said to them, "Most assuredly, I say to you, Moses did not give you the bread from heaven, but My Father gives you the true bread from heaven. For the bread of God is He who comes down from heaven and gives life to the world."
>
> Then they said to Him, "Lord, give us this bread always."
>
> And Jesus said to them, "I am the bread of life. He who comes to Me shall never hunger, and he who believes in Me shall never thirst. But I said to you that you have seen Me and yet do not believe." (John 6:32–36)

The earthly bread, the bread of this world, will pass away, but the eternal bread of heaven, which is Jesus Christ, endures forever and will bring us to the realization of our destiny, eternal life within the Kingdom. Therefore we pray, "Give us today our supra-substantial bread"—that is, Christ Himself, that we may be sustained, nourished, and nurtured even unto salvation.

We pray for God's Kingdom to come, and in doing so we utter an eschatological prayer. We offer a plea for the realization of the Kingdom of God and for the Second Coming of Christ, for the realization of the Kingdom and its final and universal establishment are the ultimate goal toward which we strive. We pray also that God's will be done even here on earth, just as it is in the Kingdom of heaven. In Gethsemane, on the night before His Passion, Jesus in His agony prayed, "O My Father, if it is possible, let this cup pass from Me; nevertheless, not as I will, but as You *will*" (Matt. 26:39). Thus we pray for the grace of God, that we may be enlightened and come to understand that alone we can do nothing. We realize that our fallen human will must be surrendered totally to the divine will, on all occasions and in all things, if we are to achieve salvation.

We pray for the forgiveness of our transgressions with an important condition—that they will be forgiven only to the extent to which we forgive those who sin against us. For if we do not forgive freely and without reservation, then neither will we be forgiven. This is a precondition for salvation. We ask that we be not led into temptation. Clearly, God Himself will not lead us into temptation. He will not set traps for us like some capricious tyrant. But it has always been the Church's teaching that because of our fallen condition and the persistent presence of the adversary, temptation is always at hand. Neither is it possible for us of our own free will and by virtue of our own personal strength to resist and overcome temptation. We always need the grace of God to overcome demonic power. We ask God not to lead us into temptation, that the trials we must endure be tempered by His mercy, that through His grace we may not fall into the irredeemable condition of rebellion and final apostasy.

We ask, therefore, that we be delivered from the clutches and destroying power of the ultimate tempter, the evil one. This is clearly the meaning of the original text, which the Greek states simply: "but deliver us from the evil one." The prayer concludes with a doxology and declaration of faith: "For Yours is the Kingdom, the power, and the glory, forever and ever!"

CHAPTER 11

The Holy Communion

WITH THE COMPLETION OF THE Lord's Prayer, the priest faces the people and blesses them.

PRIEST: *Peace be unto all.*

PEOPLE: *And with your spirit.*

PRIEST: *Let us bow our heads to the Lord.*

PEOPLE: *To You, O Lord.*

PRIEST: *We give thanks to You, O invisible King, who by Your measureless power and in the greatness of Your mercy brought all things from nonexistence into being. Look down from heaven, O Master, upon those who have bowed their heads to You; for they have not bowed to flesh and blood, but to You, the awesome God. Therefore, O Master, distribute these gifts offered to all of us for our own good according to the need of each person.*

Through the grace and compassion and love for mankind of Your only-begotten Son, with whom You are blessed, together with Your all-holy, good, and life-giving Spirit, now and ever and unto ages of ages.

PEOPLE: *Amen.*

PRIEST: *Look down, O Lord Jesus Christ our God, from Your holy dwelling place and from the glorious throne of Your kingdom; and come to sanctify us, You who sit on high with the Father and are here invisibly present with us; and make us worthy by Your mighty hand to be given Your most pure Body and precious Blood, and through us to all Your people.*

The priest now makes three small bows before the altar.

PRIEST: *O God, be gracious to me, a sinner, and have mercy on me.*

These final prayers said by the priest once again acknowledge that God is the initiator and the completer of this mystery. It is as Creator and Sustainer of life that He beckons us to come before His throne seeking His blessings and graces. For only by them are we nurtured in our spirits, and only by the sacrifice of Jesus Christ may we receive them.

The priest takes the holy Bread and raises it up, saying in a loud voice:

PRIEST: *Let us attend! Holy things for holy people!*

He then lowers the holy Bread, making with it the sign of the Cross three times. The choir and people now sing the following hymn:

CHOIR AND PEOPLE: *One is holy, One is the Lord, Jesus Christ in the glory of God the Father. Amen.*

The priest then breaks the holy Bread into four parts, with extreme care and reverence.

PRIEST: *Broken and distributed is the Lamb of God, broken but not divided; forever eaten and never consumed, but sanctifying those who partake.*

These four parts are arranged on the paten in the sign of the Cross. In this statement we recognize the eternal and infinite scope of the sacrifice of Christ—that as His death and Resurrection were for all peoples in all times and places and not limited in extent, so is the Communion of the Body and Blood. It is never exhausted but continues always. He then takes the fragment marked *IC*, makes with it the sign of the cross over the chalice, then drops it in.

PRIEST: *The fullness of the cup of the Faith, of the Holy Spirit.*

PEOPLE: *Amen.*

Then he takes the small vessel of warm water and blesses it.

PRIEST: *Blessed is the warmth of the saints, always, now and ever and unto ages of ages.*

PEOPLE: *Amen.*

We have previously seen that the mixture of water and wine symbolizes the outpouring of water and blood from Christ's side on the cross. The priest then pours some of the warm water into the chalice, making the sign of the cross as he does so.

PRIEST: *The warmth of the Faith, full of the Holy Spirit.*

PEOPLE: *Amen.*

The priest and people then recite the prayer of Communion:

PRIEST AND PEOPLE: *I believe, O Lord, and I confess that You are truly the Christ, the Son of the living God, who came into the world to save sinners, of which I am first. And I believe that this is truly Your own immaculate Body, and that this is truly Your own precious Blood. Wherefore I pray You, have mercy on me and forgive my transgressions both voluntary and involuntary, of word of deed, of knowledge and of ignorance; and make me worthy to partake without condemnation of Your immaculate Mysteries, unto the remission of my sins and unto life everlasting. Amen.*

At your Mystical Supper, O Son of God, accept me today as a communicant: for I will not speak of Your Mysteries to Your enemies, neither will I give you a kiss as did Judas; but like the thief I will confess You: remember me, O Lord, in Your Kingdom. Not unto judgment nor unto condemnation be my partaking of Your holy Mysteries, O Lord, but unto the healing of soul and body.

With this final declaration of what has been done for us, of the nature of what is before us, and of the recognition of our responsibility in partaking of it, all is prepared. The priest then bows low before the altar and says:

PRIEST: *Lo, I draw near unto Christ, our immortal King and our God.*

The people now sing the Communion hymn proper for the day while the priest and other clergy partake of Holy Communion. On Sundays the hymn is as follows:

PEOPLE: *Praise the Lord from the heavens; Praise Him in the highest. Alleluia.*

While the Communion hymn is sung, the priest partakes of the particle of the holy Bread marked *XC*, and says:

PRIEST: *The precious and holy Body of our Lord, God, and Savior Jesus Christ is given to me, the unworthy priest (name), for the remission of sins and for eternal life.*

The priest then raises the chalice and says:

PRIEST: *The precious and holy Blood of our Lord, God, and Savior Jesus Christ is given to me, the unworthy priest (name), for the remission of my sins and for eternal life.*

He then drinks from it three times. Then, having wiped his lips with the Communion cloth, the priest kisses the chalice.

PRIEST: *This has touched my lips and shall take away my iniquities and purge away my sins.*

In like manner the other clergy concelebrating partake of Communion. The priest now places the particles of the holy Bread marked *NI* and *KA* into the chalice for the Communion of the people. He then turns to face the assembly of the faithful and raises the chalice high.

PRIEST: *With fear of God and with faith and love draw near.*

Now is the very approach to the Throne, the actual experience of the Kingdom, of the eternal. We are no longer simply of the earth; we are lifted up to the very threshold of Paradise. We stand with awe, with reverence, and with profound love in anticipation of an infinite love to be conveyed to us in return. Now we approach unworthily and with trepidation, and yet with immeasurable joy in the realization of what we are about to receive and what it will do for us. Within the chalice is the life-giving Body and Blood of the Savior, broken and shed for us unto remission of sins. Here is the very vehicle of our salvation.

The people now come forward one by one to receive this immeasurable gift, this incomparable Eucharist, in humility and contrition. As each person stands before the priest and speaks his Christian name, the priest declares the joyful tidings:

PRIEST: *The servant of God (name) receives the Body and Blood of Jesus Christ for the remission of sins and for life everlasting.*

Here is the culmination of the Divine Liturgy. Here is the whole reason for this greatest act of common action and worship: that lowly human beings, with all of their imperfections and sinfulness and in the midst of the recurring discord caused by their fallen nature, may nonetheless stand for a moment outside of time at the very foot of the Throne and commune with the Infinite.

The priest takes the Communion spoon and removes from the cup a portion of the Body and Blood, which he places in the mouth of the communicant. Having thus received, the communicant makes the sign of the Cross, recalling with thanks the immense and immeasurable sacrifice given for him by the Lord on Calvary. The communicant then reverently takes a piece of the blessed bread, the unconsecrated bread that recalls the *agape* feast of the early Church. Thus it is in so simple and so intimate a manner that we are able to partake of the heavenly Mysteries under the simple appearance of food.

Co-celebration with the priest of the Divine Liturgy, with its climax in the reception of Holy Communion, is truly the greatest act that ordinary humans may perform. This is no exaggeration, for it is through this common action that heaven and earth are brought into intimate juxtaposition and that we, the helpless and sometimes hopeless, are brought to a realization of our potential for eternal peace. We have but to grasp the outstretched hand of Christ with reverence and love and turn our hearts, minds, and wills to Him. It is for this reason that frequent Holy Communion is to be urged strongly. But salvation is not automatic. The outstretched hand of Christ must be voluntarily taken. The human being must by free will rise and walk with Him and gain strength by communing and following His example. This is synergy: we work together with God, trusting in Him without question, surrendering completely to His will but taking nothing for granted.

We must work at our salvation. Calvary opened the gates of heaven, but we must desire to walk through them. Regular

Communion taken in humility, sincerity, and contrition is the greatest source of saving grace available. But we must avail ourselves of it in penitence and in a spirit of reconciliation, so that we do not turn the gift of grace from a blessing into a curse.

The Orthodox practice of receiving the Body and Blood together by spoon stems from practical considerations. Its primary purpose is to be able to give Communion to large numbers of people quickly and to ensure that they eat the Holy Gifts. (In ancient times there arose a problem with some not eating Eucharist but taking it home to use for superstitious purposes.) The practice can also be seen as a reflection of the Resurrection of Jesus Christ. In His death, the Body was broken and the Blood was spilled; in the chalice these two elements are recombined, actualizing the Resurrection. So the bread and wine, the Body and Blood, are taken together—two elements that have become one heavenly and spiritual food through the work of the Holy Spirit and that show forth the Lord's death until He comes (1 Cor. 11:26).

During the Communion of the people, the choir sings the following hymn:

> CHOIR: *Of Your Mystical Supper, O Son of God, accept me today as a communicant; I will not speak of Your Mysteries to Your enemies, neither will I give You a kiss as did Judas; but like the thief I will confess You: remember me, O Lord, in Your Kingdom.*
>
> When all the communicants have been served, the priest covers the chalice with its veil and blesses the people with it.
>
> PRIEST: *O God, save Your people and bless Your inheritance!*
>
> PEOPLE: *We have seen the true light, we have received the heavenly Spirit, we have found the true Faith, worshiping the undivided Trinity, who has saved us.*

This response, a masterpiece of understatement, expresses in small measure a conception of where we have been and what we have received. To say these words is like remarking on a beautiful sunset in order to recall the golden splendors and magnificent brilliance of noonday. Yet we are capable of nothing else. We have stood uncomprehending before God's very presence, or perhaps comprehending a little, becoming aware of the immensity of the Trinitarian glory—but finding few and inadequate words to describe it.

During this time, the priest gently wipes the remaining particles from the paten into the chalice.

> PRIEST: *O Lord, wash away the sins of all those here commemorated by Your precious Blood, through the prayers of Your saints.*
>
> Then the priest covers the chalice and censes it three times.

> PRIEST: *Be exalted, O God, above the heavens, and Your glory above all the earth.*
>
> He then takes the chalice in his right hand and the paten in his left, and turns to face the people. He raises the sacred vessels slowly, holding the chalice above the paten.

> PRIEST: *Blessed is our God, always, now and ever and unto ages of ages.*

> PEOPLE: *Amen. Let our mouths be filled with Your praise, O Lord, that we may sing of Your glory; for You have made us worthy to partake of Your Holy Mysteries. Keep us in Your holiness, that all day long we may meditate on Your righteousness. Alleluia, Alleluia, Alleluia!*

> The priest now carries the chalice and paten to the preparation table and places them upon it. He then returns to the altar, where he makes the sign of the cross with the Gospel

book. The deacon meanwhile has taken his place before the Royal Doors.

DEACON: *Let us attend! Having received the holy, most pure, immortal, heavenly, life-giving, and awesome Mysteries of Christ, let us worthily give thanks unto the Lord.*

PEOPLE: *To You, O Lord.*

We observe a solemn sequence of events from the preparation for Holy Communion to the creedal confession and the Communion of the people. The holy Bread—that is, the actual Body of Jesus Christ—is broken upon the paten, but this fraction still remains one and undivided in essence. That particle stamped with the name of Jesus (IC), which was cut from the prosphora in the Service of Preparation, is then reunited in the chalice with the precious Blood—an act that shows forth the revitalization of the crucified Christ and therefore the Resurrection. With their collective praying of the confessional prayer of the Communion, each person, clergy and laity, acknowledges their unworthiness in a personal manner. This is their confession which is addressed to Christ Himself in hope that their receipt of the Holy Gifts will not be unto condemnation, since Christ Himself instituted this very sacrament for the remission of sins and for everlasting life. At this time, the people should reverently petition the Lord in the same manner, silently, reflecting upon their own unworthiness and uniting spiritually to Christ, imploring His mercy.

The holy Bread and Wine commingled in the chalice have become for us the Body and Blood of the Lord. They have become so within the context of the Kingdom itself and serve to remind us of the Incarnation, that the Word was made flesh and dwelt among us (John 1:14). And through this remembrance of the Incarnation we must remember the world and the almost incredible fact that Christ became incarnate, suffered, and died for the life of the world. It is now, turning wholly to Christ, that we may perceive the world as it really is, the full glory of God's creation in the reality in which it was made. In Communion, Christ comes to dwell within us, and we partake of Him. Also, we are united one with another in that solidarity and total unity of love that was originally to be our condition and that the world has cast aside. No one merits Communion: no one is worthy, holy, or righteous enough by themselves to receive it. Yet this saving blessing comes to us as a free gift from God, and for this reason we refer to the sacred species—the bread and the wine that are consecrated for us—as the Holy Gifts. In the Eucharist we offer to God those very basic elements upon which our physical life depends—elements of our food and drink—and in return we receive the heavenly Bread and the heavenly Drink, which restore us and lead us to eternal life.

CHAPTER 12

The Thanksgiving

THE PRIEST NOW RECITES THE prayer of thanksgiving:

> PRIEST: *We thank You, O Sovereign Lord and lover of mankind, benefactor of our souls and bodies, that you have made us worthy today of Your heavenly and immortal Mysteries. Direct our way, strengthen all of us in Your fear, guard our life, guide our steps; through the prayers and intercessions of the glorious Theotokos and Ever-Virgin Mary and of all Your saints.*
>
> *For You are our sanctification, and we give glory to You, to the Father and to the Son and to the Holy Spirit, now and ever and unto ages of ages.*
>
> PEOPLE: *Amen.*

The mysteries are celebrated, the Communion has been consummated, and thanks have been rendered to God Almighty. We have partaken of Communion with Christ, and our communion with one another is made possible. We return to the world refreshed, perceiving this world with new reverence and wonder. For if we look, we may perceive the hand of God in all things and Christ dwelling among us and within us.

PRIEST: *Let us go forth in peace.*

PEOPLE: *In the name of the Lord.*

PRIEST: *Let us pray to the Lord.*

PEOPLE: *Lord, have mercy.*

> The priest now emerges from the sanctuary through the Royal Doors and stands facing the icon of Christ.

PRIEST: *O Lord, who bless those who praise You, and sanctify those who put their trust in You, save Your people and bless Your inheritance. Protect the whole body of Your Church, and sanctify those who love the beauty of Your house. Glorify them by Your divine power, and do not forsake us who hope in You. Give peace to Your world, to Your churches, to the priests, to all civil authorities, to the armed forces, and to all Your people. For every good and perfect gift is from above, coming down from You, the Father of Lights, and to You we ascribe glory, thanksgiving, and worship; to the Father and to the Son and to the Holy Spirit, now and ever and unto ages of ages.*

PEOPLE: *Amen. Blessed be the name of the Lord from this time forth and forever.*

This prayer is called the Prayer from the Ambon. In the primitive Church, it constituted a simple dismissal, a blessing that was probably no more than "Go in peace." Gradually, it became more elaborate and was recited in the place from which the Gospel was read. This structure, called the *ambon*, is often not seen in the churches of today, and the prayer is recited from before the icon of Christ.

The priest now returns to the sanctuary through the Royal Doors and passes to the altar.

PRIEST: *O Christ our God, who are Yourself the fulfillment of the Law and the Prophets, who accomplished all the good pleasure of the Father, fill our hearts with the joy and gladness of Your Holy Spirit, now and ever and unto ages of ages.*

PEOPLE: *Amen.*

The priest now returns to the Royal Doors and offers the final blessing.

PRIEST: *The blessing of the Lord and His mercy come upon you, through His grace and love toward mankind, always, now and ever and unto ages of ages.*

PEOPLE: *Amen.*

PRIEST: *Glory to You, O Christ, our God and our hope, glory to You.*

CHOIR AND PEOPLE: *Glory to the Father, and to the Son, and to the Holy Spirit, both now and ever and unto ages of ages. Amen. Lord have mercy, Lord have mercy, Lord have mercy. Father, bless.*

PRIEST: *May Christ our true God, who has risen from the dead, through the intercessions of His most pure and holy Mother, the holy, glorious and all-honorable apostles, Saint John Chrysostom, whose Divine Liturgy we celebrate, Saint (name), whose memory we commemorate today, Saint (patron saint of the Church), and of all the saints, have mercy on us and save us, for He is good and loves mankind.*

Through the prayers of our holy Fathers, Lord Jesus Christ our God, have mercy on us and save us.

CHOIR AND PEOPLE: *Amen.*

The journey is ended. The Divine Liturgy is over. The people come forth to reverence the cross held by the priest and to receive the blessed bread as they depart. The departure from the church might at first seem like an anticlimax. The faithful, together with their priest, have risen to the incomparable majesty of the Kingdom. At the very threshold they have partaken of the Body and Blood of the Savior. Now they must go forth from the church, from having partaken of heaven, to live out the gospel. Just as coming to church for the Divine Liturgy is a sacrament, the sacrament of gathering, so is the departure. We return to our daily lives challenged to live continually as if we were before the Throne of God, for our citizenship is there, in heaven.

A Call to Worship

Come, let us worship and bow down before God our King.

Come, let us worship and bow down before Christ, our King and our God.

Come, let us worship and bow down before Christ Himself, our King and our God.

—The call to worship

T HERE IS A MOVEMENT WITHIN Western Christianity toward liturgical worship that would especially please St. John Chrysostom, the former Bishop of Constantinople, who is honored in the name of the Divine Liturgy used almost universally within Orthodox churches today. One of the principal reasons for this is that this movement for liturgical worship evidences a return to the Scriptures and to obeying the will of God.

Liturgical worship is a return to the Scriptures because that is precisely what the Divine Liturgy is composed of and built upon. As Fr. Constantine Nasr has shown in his thorough treatment of the subject, *The Bible in the Liturgy*, virtually every element of the Divine Liturgy is taken from Scripture. He documents 729 direct references from the Bible: 216 from the Old Testament and 513 from the New Testament make up the Liturgy.[80]

Let's go back to St. John Chrysostom for a moment. He received his name posthumously. It means "John the Golden Mouth" and refers to his gift of preaching and exhortation. It is noteworthy that St. John Chrysostom, perhaps the greatest biblical expositor of all time, was the man for whom the Liturgy of the entire Church was named. The Bible man was also the worship man.

He knew the Bible, he used the Bible, he preached the Bible, he lived the Bible—and he worshiped the way the Bible and the God whom it reveals instruct us to. If we are able to distill from all of this a summary of what the early Christian Fathers from Ignatius to John Chrysostom would say the Church was to be, it would be liturgical, sacramental, episcopal, and conciliar. What is meant by these characteristics?

Liturgical

The early Fathers understood the Church to be God's own people, restored to the fellowship of the Kingdom and called to worship in the manner which He had revealed. The purpose of salvation and the focus of Christian life is communion with God. In Jesus Christ, fellowship is restored, and we may enter into His communion. But how? Does it just happen, is it mental or emotional, or is it something practical that we must work at?

Like any other relationship, this one needs work. Communion with God requires time and effort. It is not just a theoretical proposition: it is a practical one that is grounded in worship. Saint Symeon the New Theologian, an Orthodox theologian of the tenth and eleventh centuries and one of Christianity's best expositors of the spiritual life, clearly linked worship and spirituality. As abbot of a monastery in Constantinople, he was constantly challenging

---

80 Constantine Nasr, *The Bible and the Liturgy* (Oklahoma City: Nasr Publishing Co., 1988.

the monks in his charge to pursue their personal spiritual life and attend daily liturgical services.[81] The liturgical life guides the spiritual life: they are two sides of the same coin. This is true for monks, whose calling and gift is a life dedicated to communion with God, but it is true for us as well. We see in the monastic life that the celebration of the daily liturgical hours of worship coincides with the spiritual disciplines of prayer and meditation.

This commitment to the critical importance of worship has been preserved in Orthodox Christianity. The Orthodox Church has kept worship central from the beginning. It has indeed worked to enhance and beautify worship, but never at the cost of substance. It has poured its best theological content into worship, such that more theological content can be found in worship than in textbooks. The Orthodox Church has worked to make worship all that it can be, because it is in worship that the Church is brought into being. For most of us, this is where the most tangible communion with God the Blessed Trinity takes place.

Orthodox worship is real and practical. That is why Orthodox Christians know who and what they are. Historian Carl Friedrich was quoted in the November 7, 1987, issue of *Time* magazine describing the difference between the French and Americans:

To be an American is an ideal, while to be a Frenchman is a fact. A Frenchman knows what it means to be a Frenchman. Americans constantly wonder about themselves, about what they represent, about their purpose and their virtue and where they stand in the world. Americans are constantly reinventing themselves.

This speaks to the real dilemma facing much of Western Christianity, which has continued for over five hundred years to deal

---

81   Basile Krivocheine, preface to *St. Symeon the New Theologian: The Discourses*, by Symeon the New Theologian, trans. C. J. deCatanzaro (Crestwood, NY: St. Vladimir's Seminary Press), 81.

with the consequences and changes resulting from the Reformation and the Counter-Reformation. One of these consequences is that much of Western Christianity is no longer liturgical. Western Christians no longer worship as the early Church did, and they worship far less frequently. Bishop Lefebvre, who was excommunicated from the Roman Catholic Church in the late 1980s due to controversy surrounding the Society of Saint Pius X, was not all wrong. His desire to return to the historic liturgical worship of the Tridentine Mass (in spite of the problems inherent in using Latin, an ancient and dead language) is an admirable one in many ways from an Orthodox perspective.

The average Orthodox Christian knows a great deal about his or her faith. Why? Because they worship liturgically. They say what they believe. They hear what they believe. Their worship is liturgical and substantive. They hear it, say it, see it, feel it, and smell it. And because of this it is a part of them and they know it. This is not to say that there are no nominal Orthodox Christians. Rather, it is to affirm that, all things being equal, the average Orthodox Christian knows, understands, and practices his or her faith more deeply because of how they worship. Liturgical worship makes itself a part of your being and thus serves as a point of departure to deeper communion with God.

Sacramental

The early Fathers also believed that the Church is sacramental in character. And the sacramental life of the Church leads to a sacramental view of all of life: to view all things as having come from God and to offer all things back to God in thanksgiving and praise. To be in communion with God in all places, at all times, through all things. In a word, to be priestly. It is only out of this worldview that the Sacraments can be truly understood, appreciated, and experienced.

A sacramental view of life enables us to see and experience the grace of God in all things at all times. It is only then that the specific sacraments take on particular value—not because they are different from everything else, but because, having been revealed by God, they especially manifest His grace, which fills all of life. We must not set the Sacraments apart from the rest of life; rather, we must see them as the epitome of the grace that God makes available to us. They are special or sacramental because God has set these acts aside within His Church. This grace is the spiritual nurture we need to live in conformity to the will of God. And as the Eucharist is the epitome of the Sacraments, the place to receive it is in the Divine Liturgy, that worship whose whole purpose is to move us to the Kingdom of God, that we might partake of the Body and Blood of Jesus Christ.

Episcopal

The episcopal character of the Church flows from the liturgical and the sacramental. At the very least the episcopacy is a protective and guiding role, ensuring that the things we have from God will continue unchanged, as God is unchanging, and that we continue to be Orthodox, to practice correctly what was given to us in the beginning.

This is the Way that the Lord established. He called the Twelve. They became the apostles after the Resurrection and Ascension—the ruling elders of the Church. As the Church grew, so did its responsibilities; hence the expansion from the apostles to the bishops, who have always been understood to be the servants, the caretakers of the Church. And of course this episcopate guided and directed the Church as it continued to grow and encounter problems not addressed in the New Testament Church. Modern Christianity has given lip service to the early Church, and seminaries are full of quests for the New Testament Church. But to what end? The New Testament is full of teaching on the Church and on worship, but how much of it is put into practice? As a

Protestant, I had to ask myself, when was the last time I was ill and called for the elders of the church and let them pray over me, anointing me with oil in the name of the Lord (see James 5:14)? Or how frequently did any clergyman I knew worship and pray in the daily manner of the New Testament Church?

Jesus called the Twelve purposefully, and the episcopal character of the Church may be traced in an unbroken line from the present back to these apostles. I was chrismated by a priest who was ordained by a bishop. He in turn had been ordained by a bishop, who had been ordained by a bishop, who had been ordained by a bishop—and so on, back to St. Peter, who established the episcopate of Antioch and who was called and ordained by Jesus Christ. That is remarkable historic continuity. In addition to continuity, authority is an essential aspect of this tradition, for without episcopal authority, there is chaos. Christ's Church needs both authority and continuity with its past, perhaps more today than ever before.

Conciliar

Finally, for the early Fathers the Church was fundamentally conciliar. This aspect of the Church speaks of both unity and equality. From the beginning, the bishops operated in a collegial fashion. No one ruled over all the others; rather, all were equal and united in and by Jesus Christ. This collegiality was not always easy to maintain: it was marked at times by tension and infighting. Nevertheless, all struggled together to determine the will of God. For a thousand years the struggle was seen as worthwhile— it was for the continued unity of the Body of Christ. And it was the Body that suffered when the conciliar unity was broken.

Somehow, inextricably, these four attributes of the Church are bound together. We must have them all. If we remove one, it affects the whole, as is illustrated by break in communion between the Eastern and Western Church. Granted, there were hundreds of years of theological and political developments that led to this, but in the schism that occurred in AD 1054 the conciliar character of the Church lost out to greed and the hunger for power. It was jettisoned by Rome in favor of autocracy.

The historical anomaly of the Dark Ages and the medieval period, with its reversion to the primitive and superstitious, and the consequent halt of any cultural, political, or religious progress, delayed the inevitable loss of the other characteristics in the Western Church. But it bred a new set of problems: graft, political intrigue, and spiritual rot, which resulted in the Reformation and various attempts at reforming within the Roman Catholic Church as well. To be sure, Orthodox Christianity had its own set of problems under the autocratic rule of both the Byzantine and Ottoman Empires. But they were different problems, occurring in isolation from those going on in the West and in some ways fostering the maintenance of the best characteristics of the Church. This was in contrast to the political process in the West, which encouraged their disintegration.

According to Protestant theologian Bernard Ramm, it was the Enlightenment, which took place during the eighteenth century, that made for the most dramatic changes in Western Christianity.[82] It was this Age of Reason, he contends, that was responsible for the radical secularization of Europe. One significant effect was the replacement of the understanding of the state as a divine institution paralleling the Church with an understanding of the state as grounded in a social contract. Additionally, education came to be grounded on humanistic presuppositions. Those types of radical and widespread social changes affect every person at the deepest levels of their lives. Ramm cites a list of words that would be disapproved of by the Enlightenment: "authority, antiquity, tradition,

---

82   Bernard Ramm, *After Fundamentalism: The Future of Evangelical Theology* (San Francisco: Harper & Row, 1983).

church, revelation, supernatural, and theological explanations."[83]

The radical tenets of the Enlightenment changed Western society and Western theology, and thus the way Western Christians (Protestant and Catholic) thought and worshiped. It is important to note, however, that much of the Enlightenment was also beneficial. Out of it came modern science, improved social and economic conditions, and much more. However, Ramm specifically states that the crisis in modern theology can be traced back to the fact that Western Christianity never came to grips with the consequences of the Enlightenment. Rather, the Western Church absorbed much of what the Enlightenment taught without question, and much of it is contrary to biblical Christianity.

Following on the heels of the Enlightenment, the inevitable began to happen in the West. Having lost the conciliar, out of which sprung the Church's unity, the Roman Catholic Church began to lose the liturgical and sacramental. It was perhaps due to the hierarchical episcopal structure that the liturgical and the sacramental were held together for so long. The nadir of this process was Vatican II. There, the traditionally sacred was replaced with the secular, and we have seen the consequent weakening of the sacramental and an incipient revolt against the episcopal in the ensuing years. All of this is illustrated, within the Roman Catholic Church at least, by Bishop Lefebvre's revolt.

Following the Reformation, Protestants made swift and sweeping changes. In their haste to clean house of all things Roman, they threw out much that was biblical as well. The first to go was the episcopacy. This was motivated in part by a desire to remove corrupt bishops; however, it was contrary to the New Testament and fifteen hundred years of Christian practice. Those Protestant churches that didn't do away with the episcopacy modified it so much that it was barely distinguishable.

For the rest of Protestantism in the generations following

---

83 Ramm, 3.

Luther and Calvin, much of the sacramental and liturgical began to dissolve as well. Then, as the Enlightenment swept through Europe, Protestantism began to accept many of its propositions. When authority, tradition, the Church, revelation, and the supernatural all go, what is left? The result is modern Protestantism, a loose confederation of churches where, as recent history shows, most anything goes. And none of its churches would be recognizable as the Church to St. John Chrysostom.

In the past century, with the episcopal and sacramental gone, and with Protestantism striving to be relevant to this world, most of the liturgical has likewise been replaced with the personal or the secular, thus the current state of affairs, where so little of today's worship corresponds with worship in the early Christian Church. In a sense, this situation makes the present surging interest in liturgical worship appear odd. On further consideration, though, it is only natural. For mankind was created in the image of God, and man is a liturgical creature by nature. Hold back water or food, and even the most estranged child begins to come closer.

This current interest in liturgical worship involves more than just the desire for correct form, for the proper things to do and say. It expresses the deeper need we all have for the sacramental, for the spiritual nurture that God alone can provide. It can be likened to seeking an answer to the question "Where's the beef?" Many Americans remember this slogan, made popular by both hamburger advertisements and the 1984 presidential campaign. Why did this campaign work? Because it struck an inner cord about substance. Were we receiving substance in exchange for our money? Were the programs and rhetoric we were being told to accept substantive, or were they just empty words? We can ask the same question about our spiritual lives: Is there substance? The type of sacramental substance that makes liturgical worship a thing of the Kingdom?

As we have seen, this sacramental experience is more than just the Eucharist. It is much more like an onion, composed of many layers of spiritual reality, at the center of which is the Eucharist. To reap the true benefit from the Sacraments, we must be sacramental in our outlook and in our living. This is what is really behind the current movement toward liturgical worship. It is as if the whole historical process were reversing itself. The liturgical movement confirms that Western Christianity has strayed from liturgical worship, but it also illustrates that in the process it has lost the sacramental reality, the "beef," on which the liturgical was founded.

Again, it should be stated that the Eastern Orthodox Church remained true to its origins in part because of the isolation it experienced under the Ottoman Turks. The consequences of the Enlightenment did not sweep through the Orthodox churches, undercutting the biblical worldview and the sacramental understanding of life. In Russia the Orthodox Church was established in AD 988, and for most of its life it existed in a society that was isolated from the West. Notwithstanding the attempts of many Russian emperors to westernize their society, for the vast majority of average Russians, Russia has always maintained its distinctive identity. And the same is true for the Russian Orthodox Church. The Orthodox Church did develop a unique set of problems because of its circumstances, the worst of which is nationalism. But the important point is that because the experience was different, the result was different.

It is our hope and prayer that this historical process in the West—with all of its consequences—has reached an end, especially as concerns liturgical worship and the Sacraments. We trust that the current interest in liturgical worship and in Orthodox Christianity signals a return to the true fundamentals of the Faith—those things that have been taught consistently from the beginning and that made it possible for the early Church to claim the world for God and then transform it.

The current resurgence of Orthodoxy in North America offers a twofold opportunity to Christians. For Protestants, the opportunity is to finish the Reformation—as it should have been done—by returning to the Church that has kept the apostolic faith. May the endless Orthodox-Protestant dialogue turn to change of mind and movement. For Roman Catholics, who are separated from their Orthodox brethren over theological issues made worse by political differences, Orthodoxy offers the same opportunity of unity—the reuniting of the Church as it was originally created and structured: One, Holy, Catholic, and Apostolic. Further, in this post-Vatican II era, Orthodoxy continues the liturgical worship that has been lost to the modernization of so many Catholic parishes.

The second opportunity operates at a personal level. It is simply the opportunity to come home, to enter into the fullness of the Faith—theologically, sacramentally, and liturgically. Come home to the fullness of the Faith as it was revealed in Jesus Christ and manifested in the early Church. This call is made in all humility—not in a judgmental fashion—by two Christians who have struggled over the years with the lack of fulfillment to be found in their early Christian lives. We have found in Orthodoxy the fullness, the completeness that can only be described as "coming home."

Let us return to a mindset for worship. Let us commit ourselves to set our hearts on worship. It was God's revelation for us, that in it we might find ourselves and be fulfilled as His children. As much as anything, this book is a call to worship—to a return to Orthodox Christianity as the "right worship" initiated by the revelation of God in the Old Testament and solidified in the early Church.

It is by having been to the Kingdom and having worshiped at the throne of God, by experiencing the joy and communion to be found there, that we are enabled to live. Let us set our eyes on that goal, so that we may observe upon leaving the church service that we have worshiped, that we have been to heaven, that we have been fed. We invite you to experience Orthodox Christianity. Attend the Divine Liturgy at an Orthodox Church, for this more than anything else will confirm to you, in your spirit, what we have found to be true.

About the Authors

BENJAMIN D. WILLIAMS holds a Master of Theology from Fuller Theological Seminary (1979). He has served in various facets of Christian ministry, including as pastor, cantor, prison chaplain, and parish council chairman. He has been actively involved in the founding of three mission parishes and was ordained as a reader (OCA) in 1994. He has served in various leadership roles in non-profit organizations and has conducted leadership development seminars for the past twenty years.

The late HAROLD B. ANSTALL was, until his retirement, Professor of Pathology at the University of Utah Medical Center and author of many scientific books and publications. He was also a lay theologian in the area of liturgical worship and liturgical theology, part of a venerable tradition in the Eastern Orthodox Churches. Harry regularly taught adult education classes, particularly in the area of liturgics, over the years in various Orthodox churches in Salt Lake City, UT.

Milton Keynes UK
Ingram Content Group UK Ltd.
UKHW011842120424
441050UK00004B/254

9 781944 967543